# HYPNOTHERAPY:
# A Modern Approach

# Pergamon Titles of Related Interest

**Barber/Spanos/Chaves** HYPNOSIS, IMAGINATION AND HUMAN POTENTIALITIES
**Ellis/McInerney/DiGiuseppe/Yeager** RATIONAL-EMOTIVE THERAPY WITH ALCOHOLICS AND SUBSTANCE ABUSERS
**Weiss** DREAM ANALYSIS IN PSYCHOTHERAPY

# Related Journals *

CLINICAL PSYCHOLOGY REVIEW
JOURNAL OF ANXIETY DISORDERS

*Free sample copies available upon request

**PSYCHOLOGY PRACTITIONER GUIDEBOOKS**

**EDITORS**

**Arnold P. Goldstein,** Syracuse University
**Leonard Krasner,** Stanford University & SUNY at Stony Brook
**Sol L. Garfield,** Washington University

# HYPNOTHERAPY:
# A Modern Approach

**WILLIAM L. GOLDEN**
Institute for Rational-Emotive Therapy and
Cornell Medical College

**E. THOMAS DOWD**
Kent State University

**FRED FRIEDBERG**
Nassau Pain and Stress Center

**PERGAMON PRESS**
New York . Oxford . Beijing . Frankfurt
São Paulo . Sydney . Tokyo . Toronto

| U.S.A. | Pergamon Press, Maxwell House, Fairview Park, Elmsford, New York 10523, U.S.A. |
| U.K. | Pergamon Press, Headington Hill Hall, Oxford OX3 0BW, England |
| PEOPLE'S REPUBLIC OF CHINA | Pergamon Press, Room 4037, Qianmen Hotel, Beijing, People's Republic of China |
| FEDERAL REPUBLIC OF GERMANY | Pergamon Press, Hammerweg 6, D-6242 Kronberg, Federal Republic of Germany |
| BRAZIL | Pergamon Editora, Rua Eca de Queiros, 346, CEP 04011, Paraiso, São Paulo, Brazil |
| AUSTRALIA | Pergamon Press Australia, P.O. Box 544, Potts Point, N.S.W. 2011, Australia |
| JAPAN | Pergamon Press, 8th Floor, Matsuoka Central Building, 1-7-1 Nishishinjuku, Shinjuku-ku, Tokyo 160, Japan |
| CANADA | Pergamon Press Canada, Suite No. 271, 253 College Street, Toronto, Ontario, Canada M5T 1R5 |

First edition 1987

Library of Congress Cataloging-in-Publication Data

Golden, William L.
Hypnotherapy: a modern approach.
(Psychology practitioner guidebooks)
Includes index.
1. Hypnotism – Therapeutic use.   I. Dowd,
E. Thomas.   II. Friedberg, Fred.   III. Title.
IV. Series.   [DNLM: 1. Hypnosis – methods.
WM 415 G618h]
RC495.G57   1987        615.8'512        87-2480
ISBN 0-08-034303-1 Hardcover
ISBN 0-08-034302-3 Flexicover

*Printed in Great Britain by A. Wheaton & Co. Ltd., Exeter*

# Dedication

We dedicate this book to those disparate theoreticians and practitioners who have influenced each of us and this book in many ways: Albert Ellis and Milton Erickson. Although they approach psychotherapy in radically different ways, they are alike in their willingness to challenge prevailing modes of thought and in their profound respect for their clients.

# Table of Contents

FOREWORD by Daniel Araoz     ix

PREFACE     xi

ACKNOWLEDGEMENTS     xiii

Chapter

1. INTRODUCTION     1

2. HYPNOTIC INDUCTION     8

3. DEPRESSION     30

4. HYPNOTHERAPY FOR FEARS, PHOBIAS, AND STRESS-RELATED DISORDERS     45

5. HYPNOTHERAPEUTIC PAIN CONTROL     58

6. HABIT DISORDERS     74

7. TREATMENT OF SEXUAL DYSFUNCTION     85

8. OVERCOMING RESISTANCE IN HYPNOTHERAPY     100

9. SELF-HYPNOSIS TRAINING     119

AFTERWORD     137

APPENDIX     139

REFERENCES                                              142

AUTHOR INDEX                                            147

SUBJECT INDEX                                           149

ABOUT THE AUTHORS                                       151

PSYCHOLOGY PRACTITIONER GUIDEBOOKS                      152

# Foreword

With the current plethora of books on hypnosis, I asked myself what this volume had to offer. After reading it carefully, I can truly say that Golden, Dowd, and Friedberg, have accomplished two important tasks for the present development of hypnosis. First, with scientific care they validate the nontraditional approach to clinical hypnosis. Even though much has been published since the early 1970s on the modern approach to hypnotherapy, one often misses the factual validation that comes from research. Golden, Dowd, and Friedberg are careful to list as much of modern studies as possible, to justify clinical procedures using hypnosis.

The second task is to add to the demystification of clinical hypnosis. Without being iconoclastic, they depart from traditional hypnosis. In thus departing (coming close to what I have described as the *New Hypnosis*), they still keep structural elements that are useful guides for hypnosis tyros. However, in departing from traditional, laboratory conceived methods of using hypnosis, Golden, Dowd and Friedberg force us to honestly question the dogmatic posture that for several decades has wanted to restrict the use of hypnosis to a handful of elitist professions. If hypnosis is "naturalistic" and at the reach of any normally functioning individual, should we not teach everybody self-hypnosis? Shouldn't teachers, managers, sports coaches, and others dealing directly with people learn hypnotic principles?

By demystifying hypnosis, Golden, Dowd, and Friedberg pragmatically redefine hypnosis as one of many different thinking modalities that can be learned and enhanced for people's enrichment and happiness. This book presents the nontraditional use of hypnosis as scientifically valid and one that can be learned.

This is not to say that the authors disregard the professional cautions proper to any intervention aimed at helping people change. On the contrary, their professionalism is evident throughout the book, both in not making unrealistic claims for hypnotherapy and in warning those who want to use this method of the need to understand and master it.

Foreword

It is with pleasure that I welcome this new volume to the growing literature of the New Hypnosis. It is with high regard that I encourage clinicians to read and assimilate what this book has to offer. I have been professionally enriched by Golden, Dowd, and Friedberg's *Hypnotherapy: a modern approach*.

Daniel L Araoz, Ed D, ABPP,ABPH
Professor of Mental Health Counseling
Long Island University

# Preface

Hypnosis, or what was earlier called Mesmerism, has waxed and waned in popularity over the last few centuries. Currently we are witnessing an explosive rebirth of interest in the field, and new books seem to come out weekly. This very interest is fraught with danger, however, in that we risk overselling the power of hypnosis as a tool for psychological change. It could have been this very uncritical enthusiasm that previously contributed to its periodic eclipses. Therefore, it is important that hypnosis be used in a responsible fashion by therapists, not as a therapy itself but as an adjunctive technique to therapy. It is this view of hypnosis as a technique to be integrated into psychotherapy when appropriate that this book has attempted to foster.

We have called our approach *Modern Hypnotherapy* because it includes the newer cognitive–behavioral and Ericksonian methods and the more traditional uses of hypnosis. A theme of the book, however, is that hypnosis is a coping strategy clients can learn to use for their benefit in a variety of problematic situations. This echoes the view that, in the final analysis, all hypnosis is self-hypnosis. Thus, far from being a powerful and mysterious technique foisted upon a hapless client by an all-powerful therapist, hypnosis is a method that requires the active collaboration of the client to achieve any results at all. Although such a view of hypnosis might be disappointing to those who long for magical answers to life's traumas, it could help insure that hypnosis does not once again suffer an eclipse from being oversold by its adherents.

This book has been designed so that the practitioner with little knowledge of hypnosis can learn to use it in the treatment of a variety of psychological problems. The first chapters provide an overview of the field and several methods of hypnotic induction. Another chapter presents a hypno-therapeutic view of client resistance, along with strategies for overcoming it. The majority of the chapters offer detailed methods of using hypnosis in treating a variety of problems. Case examples are used liberally throughout the book to illustrate how these techniques can actually be applied. However, it is important that the reader see these cases as illustrative only, not as prescriptive. They do not define the only correct way of using hypnosis in psychotherapy, but only one way. Therapist flexibility and adaptability remain as important here as in any therapeutic approach.

It is also important that the reader view this book as a first step only, not as a final destination. If you intend to use hypnosis seriously in your work, it is important that you obtain additional training, both in the form of attendance at workshops and through additional reading. Fortunately there are a large number of excellent workshops being presented, and the number of books is increasing constantly. Thus, the serious student of hypnosis should lack no resources.

We hope that you enjoy this "therapeutic odyssey."

W.G.
E.T.D.
F.F.

# Acknowledgements

Material from *Hypnotherapy : An exploratory casebook* by Milton H. Erickson and Ernest L Rossi, coypright 1979 by Ernest L Rossi, reprinted with permission from Irvington Publishers, Inc., 740 Broadway, New York, N Y 10003.

Material from *Hypnotic realities* by Milton H. Erickson, Ernest L. Rossi, and Sheila Rossi, copyright 1976 by Ernest L. Rossi, reprinted with permission from Irvington Publishers, Inc.

Material from *The collected papers of Milton H. Erickson on Hypnosis* edited by Ernest L. Rossi, copyright 1980 by Ernest Rossi, reprinted with permission from Irvington Publishers, Inc.

Material from *Uncommon therapy: The Psychiatric Techniques of Milton Erickson, M.D.* by Jay Haley, copyright 1973 by Jay Haley, reprinted with permission from W.W. Norton & Company, Inc., 500 Fifth Avenue. New York, N Y 10110.

Material from *An integration of Ericksonian and cognitive-behavioral hypnotherapy in the treatment of anxiety disorders* by William L. Golden in *Case studies in hypnotherapy* edited by E. Thomas Dowd and James Healy, copyright 1986 by The Guilford Press, reprinted with permission from Guilford Publications, Inc. 200 Park Avenue, South, New York, N Y 10003.

# Chapter 1

# Introduction

The purpose of *Hypnotherapy: A Modern Approach* is to show the reader how to induce and utilize clinical hypnosis. It is written for the clinician who might or might not have had previous training in or knowledge of treating clients with hypnosis. Hypnotic induction and treatment are broken down into step-by-step procedures. Transcripts of hypnotic induction procedures, therapeutic suggestions, and therapist-client interactions are provided throughout the book. The focus is on clinical techniques. Case examples are cited for the purpose of demonstrating the use of hypnotic methods.

## HYPNOTHERAPEUTIC APPROACHES

Our clinical framework is based on the integration of current and traditional hypnotherapeutic methods. For instance, clients are occasionally treated with a combination of cognitive-behavioral and Ericksonian methods. We will now acquaint the reader with each of the hypnotherapeutic approaches that have influenced us.

*Traditional Hypnotherapy.* The goal of traditional hypnotherapy is to provide symptom relief through direct suggestion. A traditional hypnotist, for example, might offer the hypnotized patient the following instruction for pain alleviation: "By the time I count to ten, your pain will completely disappear."Also, the hypnotist might use guided imagery, such as directing the client to experience a powerful anesthesia involving sensations of numbness and lessening of pain. Self-hypnosis might be taught, although such active client participation is not required. Furthermore, most traditional hypnotists attempt to achieve symptom reduction without exploring the underlying causes of the symptoms.

However, a number of the traditional hypnotherapists (Bernheim, 1895; Prince & Coriat, 1907) found that insight-oriented methods based on

1

persuasion, reasoning, and reeducation were sometimes necessary to achieve symptom alleviation. Their emphasis on rational reevaluation (cognitive restructuring) often involved hypnotic suggestions to alter the thinking patterns associated with clinical symptoms.

*Hypnoanalysis.* Freud (1920) questioned the efficacy of direct suggestion in hypnotherapy and concluded that

> It could be employed in certain cases only and not in others; with some much could be achieved by it, and with others very little, one never knew why. But worse than its capricious nature was the lack of permanence in the results; after a time, if one heard from the patient again, the old malady reappeared or had been replaced by another. (1920, p.157)

Freud's sharp criticism did not prevent some of his students from incorporating hypnosis into psychotherapy. The resulting *hypnoanalysis* combined hypnotic techniques with psychoanalysis. It was thought that hypnosis could directly tap the unconscious and therefore hasten the psychoanalytic process of uncovering and interpreting resistances, defenses, dreams, and transference.

Furthermore, standard analytic methods, such as free association and dream interpretation, were thought to be more productive under hypnosis. For example, hypnotic suggestions could induce dreams and increase dream recall and understanding. The shortened and more productive treatment under hypnoanalysis is based on the assumption that hypnosis allows the clinician to communicate directly with the unconscious mind of the client, thereby facilitating the recovery of unconscious material. Ultimately, the working through and resolution of unconcious conflicts provides the foundation for enduring therapeutic change.

"Modern hypnotherapy" focuses on both insight and symptom relief. In contrast with hypnoanalysis, it draws "insight" from awareness of maladaptive cognitions such as negative self-suggestions and their effects on emotions and behavior. These self-defeating cognitions are what psychoanalysts might have referred to as *preconscious material,* that is thoughts capable of becoming conscious. In addition to the retrieval of deeply unconscious material, hypnoanalytic techniques such as age regression and heightened recall can assist in identifying maladaptive thoughts, attitudes, and beliefs.

*Ericksonian Hypnotherapy.* Both traditional and Ericksonian methods (Erickson & Rossi, 1979) focus on symptom relief rather than on client insight into a problem. Unlike with hypnoanalysis, no efforts are made in either model to overcome early unconscious conflicts. Also, Erickson differed with traditional hypnotists in his preference for *indirect* suggestions, which he believed were less likely to mobilize client resistance.

To minimize client awareness of suggestions and possible resistance to them, indirect suggestions such as paradoxical instructions are presented. For example, the Ericksonian therapist is likely to instruct (paradoxically) the oppositional client to continue to resist, as a strategy to obtain compliance.

In one such case, a resistant client responded to an initial hypnotic induction by opening his eyes in midsuggestion and declaring "It's not working." The therapist utilized this statement by agreeing with the client and further asserting that the next attempt at hypnosis *would probably fail as well*. The client protested that the therapist was giving up on him. Assuring him that he was not, the therapist successfully induced hypnosis on the second attempt, with little change in the induction procedure.

An important Ericksonian concept that describes the interactive process between therapist and client is called *pacing and leading*. The therapist is *pacing* an individual when suggestions match the patient's ongoing behavior and experiences. As the patient becomes receptive to pacing, the hypnotist can *lead* and become more directive. For example, the therapist might pace the client by saying "as you exhale" as the client exhales and then lead by adding "you will begin to relax."

*The Hypnobehavioral Model.* Salter (1949) explained hypnosis in Pavlovian terms: He hypothesized that words are classically conditioned stimuli that elicit the conditioned response of hypnosis. Salter's clinical applications of hypnosis included counterconditioning of fears and phobias and training clients to use positive self-suggestions. His methods resemble current cognitive and behavioral methods such as relaxation training, desensitization, and cognitive restructuring.

Kroger and Fezler (1976) have also integrated hypnosis with behavior therapy techniques. Because hypnotherapeutic procedures and behavior therapy techniques are very similar (Weitzenhoffer, 1972), a natural integration can be made between the two approaches. For example, relaxation techniques and imagery are common to both hypnosis and behavior therapy.

*Cognitive–behavioral Hypnotherapy (CBH).* CBH is a generic term for cognitive–behavioral approaches to hypnotherapy. CBH methods are based on the premise that most psychological disturbance results from a destructive type of self-hypnosis that has been termed *negative self-hypnosis* by Araoz (1981, 1982, 1985). He explained that negative thinking and imagining are hypnoticlike when they are accepted without critical evaluation. The CBH client is shown how the content of negative self-hypnosis, self-defeating thoughts and images, can be changed through the corrective process of positive self-hypnosis. The client thus learns how to control the self-hypnotic process.

For example, self-defeating thoughts such as "I can't stop smoking; I'll always be hooked on cigarettes" are suggestions that interfere with the client's efforts to stop smoking. Associated self-suggestions such as "I failed; therefore I'm a weakling" can engender feelings of hopelessness. Clients are taught how to substitute more constructive self-suggestions for these negative ones, such as; "I can stop smoking cigarettes; I'm learning greater self-control." They are further told to repeat these positive suggestions during self-hypnosis practice and in real-life problem situations. The clinician then explains that prior hypnotic induction is unnecessary for therapeutic self-suggestions to be successful whenever the client needs immediate assistance such as to reduce anxiety or cravings to smoke or overeat.

*Hypnotic-skills training.* The hypnotic skills training concept is based on the premise that hypnotic suggestibility is a learnable skill rather than an unmodifiable trait. The client learns to respond to suggestion through skills training procedures that include modeling; instruction in how to think and imagine along with suggestions; thought-stopping techniques to block out distracting thoughts such as "I can't do it"; and shaping methods that reinforce the subject to stepwise improvements in hypnotic responsiveness. Research on hypnotic performance (e.g., Diamond, 1974, 1977; Gargiulo, 1983, Katz, 1979) suggests that (a) Hypnotic ability is normally distributed in the population, with some subjects possessing excellent hypnotic ability, some possessing almost none, and the majority in the middle; (b) hypnotic ability *can* be modified through hypnotic skills training (a transcript of hypnotic skills training can be found in chapter 2); and (c) most hypnotherapeutic interventions require only light to medium trance, so that excellent hypnotic ability is not necessary.

# MODERN HYPNOTHERAPY: AN INTEGRATED APPROACH

We will now integrate the previously summarized models of hypnosis into a highly pragmatic clinical approach. We will identify important similarities in underlying concepts and therapeutic techniques. Throughout the book, hypnotherapeutic methods from the various approaches will be selected and applied for maximum therapeutic effects. We subscribe to an approach best described as *technical eclecticism*. In technical eclecticism, the clinician borrows techniques freely from diverse therapeutic approaches without necessarily accepting the theories from which the techniques were derived.

*Cooperation and Motivation.* As diverse as the conceptual models appear to be, there is a significant degree of agreement about the subject variables that influence hypnotic performance. One of the most important factors common to most of the major models of hypnosis is the willingness of the subject to cooperate with the hypnotist (Spanos & Barber, 1974). Reviews of the theoretical and empirical literature exploring factors related to hypnotic performance (Spanos & Barber, 1974, 1976) have confirmed the importance of cooperation and motivation of the subject. More recently, Araoz (1981, 1982, 1985) has also endorsed the importance of client motivation in his *New Hypnosis* model.

However, there are forms of clinical hypnosis that might not depend upon conscious cooperation of the client. For instance, Erickson's indirect techniques do not seem to depend on the client's awareness or cooperation. In clinical practice, it is important for the hypnotherapist to recognize that hypnotic techniques must be individualized for the client, which can involve drawing upon techniques from more than one conceptual model. Whenever possible, we attempt to enlist the conscious cooperation of the client. When conscious cooperation is not possible, perhaps due to anxiety or resistance, we employ indirect methods.

*Thinking and Imagining.* In addition to subject cooperation Spanos and Barber (1974) concluded, in their review of the commonalities among the major conceptual models of hypnosis, that the subject's level of involvement in suggestion-related thoughts and images strongly influences hypnotic performance. Similarly, the cognitive-behavioral hypnotherapist assumes a direct causal link between cognitions or self-suggestions and emotional and behavioral consequences. For example, if one wanted a subject to experience taste, the subject might be instructed to imagine eating his or her favorite food.

Erickson has also described how cognitive processes are involved in hypnosis. He invoked the concept of *ideodynamic processes* to describe how ideas, thoughts, and images are transformed into sensory and perceptual alterations, emotional reactions, motor behavior, dreams, and so on (Erickson & Rossi, 1979). For example, an ideosensory suggestion would be "a cool breeze can make one feel gentle, tingling sensations on the skin." An ideomotor suggestion for arm levitation would be "most people can experience one hand as being lighter than the other."

Whereas the cognitive-behavioral hypnotherapist teaches the client to be aware of the link between thoughts and feelings and of how to control them, the Ericksonian hypnotherapist utilizes indirect suggestion and the client's natural ability to transform thoughts into feelings without being aware of the process. Rather than suggesting (directly) that the subject experience taste, as the cognitive-behavioral hypnotherapist might, the Ericksonian therapist constructs an indirect suggestion to produce an ideosensory phenomenon: "Some people can imagine their food so well that they can actually taste it" (Erickson & Rossi, 1979, p.23). Whether direct or indirect, both the cognitive-behavioral and Ericksonian suggestions provide the client with a productive cognitive strategy.

It is our view that many forms of psychopathology are at least partly the result of negative self-suggestions, or, negative self-hypnosis. Many of the techniques offered in this book are designed to help clients become aware of these negative cognitions and change them.

*Similarities of Technique.* In addition to similar theoretical premises, there are clinical techniques common to the models.

Suggestions and imagery are the fundamental tools that create and sustain a hypnotic state. Furthermore, imagery and suggestion are often used to identify and treat clinical problems; for instance, imagery can be used to prepare clients for coping with anxiety producing situations. Another pervasively used technique is relaxation, which is part of most hypnotic induction procedures. One exception, *alert hypnosis* used in the treatment of depression, will be discussed in chapter 3.

Two similar clinical techniques, Erickson's *pacing* and *leading* and the behavioral method of successive approximations, are both designed to reinforce clients for stepwise progress and to encourage further improvements. With successive approximations, the therapist encourages and reinforces whatever small steps the client takes toward reaching a particular goal. For instance, the initial goal for a client with sexual performance anxiety would be to become more comfortable with nonthreatening touching and caressing. Therapy would then proceed gradually to more intimate sexual contacts.

These graduated techniques require that the hypnotherapist proceed at a pace that is comfortable and acceptable to the client, rather than possibly overwhelming the client with suggestions that represent an insurmountable "leap."

*Indications for Hypnotherapy.* Our clinical experience suggests that hypnosis is generally indicated for clients who state a preference for it. When the therapist honors a client's request for hypnosis, rather than offering an alternative treatment, the likelihood of success is increased. Similarly, for clients opposed to hypnosis, we would not recommend it. Hypnotic therapy presented to a hesitant individual will likely interfere with client trust and progress. We also advise vigilance with severely paranoid individuals. Even when requesting hypnosis, these clients might exhibit paranoia about their minds being controlled by the clinician. To reduce this possibility, we advise emphasizing client *self*-control of the hypnotic process.

Wadden and Anderton (1982) reviewed the experimental research on clinical hypnosis applications and found that traditional hypnosis is most effective for asthma and clinical pain. In a later literature summary of therapeutic hypnosis and relaxation treatments, Barber (1984) concluded that hypnotherapeutic interventions are particularly effective for relief of migraine and tension headaches, insomnia, and hypertension.

In contrast, traditional hypnotic therapies for "bad habits" such as obesity, smoking, and alcoholism have shown disappointing results. We have found that hypnosis can be effective for many clinical problems, such as anxiety and phobias, sexual disorders, depression, pain, and even habit disorders when it is integrated in the manner described throughout this book.

To summarize, hypnotherapy shows a broad range of applicability to clinical problems. Most hypnotherapeutic approaches are relatively brief forms of treatment and are oriented toward symptom relief. In our view, therapeutic results are more enduring if symptom amelioration includes the modification of thoughts, feelings, and behavior patterns that maintain the symptoms.

# Chapter 2
# Hypnotic Induction

## WHAT IS TRANCE?

Some theorists claim that trance is not an important aspect of hypnosis, whereas others believe that it is. For our purposes, it is unnecessary to resolve this issue. A prominent research group (see Barber, 1979; Barber, Spanos, & Chaves, 1974) has demonstrated that formal hypnotic induction procedures involving suggestions for relaxation or drowsiness are not always needed for subjects to experience phenomena such as age regression, amnesia, catalepsy, hand levitation, and analgesia. Nevertheless, some people seem to be more responsive to suggestions after first undergoing hypnotic-trance-induction procedures that make them feel relaxed or drowsy. Furthermore, even though formal hypnotic induction is unnecessary for producing certain phenomena in experimental investigations of hypnosis, it is still what clients expect as part of hypnotherapy. Theodore X. Barber, who is the leading nontrance theorist, emphasizes the importance of expectations as one of the major factors in determining an individual's response to suggestions. This is probably the reason why, in his clinical practice of hypnosis, Barber employs hypnotic induction procedures (Barber, 1984).

There is a great deal of individual difference in the way hypnosis is experienced. Some people feel drowsy, whereas others feel alert. Many people report that they simply feel relaxed. What a person experiences during hypnosis seems to depend upon the wording of the suggestions used during the induction procedure, as well as upon what the individual expects to feel during hypnosis. If you want a client to feel relaxed during hypnosis, then suggest relaxation as part of the induction. If you want the client to feel drowsy, suggest sleepiness. If however, you want the client to experience a more energetic state, then you will be interested in a phenomenon called *alert hypnosis*. Athletes and other sportsminded individuals have used alert hypnosis for strength and endurance. It can also be used to lift a depressed mood. A detailed presentation of how to induce and utilize alert hypnosis in the treatment of depression can be found in chapter 3.

# STAGES OF HYPNOTHERAPY

Hypnotic treatment can be subdivided into five stages: (a) preparation of the client for hypnosis, (b) hypnotic induction, (c) deepening of techniques, (d) utilization of hypnosis for therapeutic purposes, and (e) termination of hypnosis. We will now describe what takes place during each of these stages.

## Preparation of the Client for Hypnosis

Preparation for hypnosis involves the establishment of rapport, the assessment of the client's problems, the clarification of misconceptions about hypnosis, and, depending on the particular approach taken by the hypnotherapist, either the testing for hypnotic susceptibility or the teaching of hypnotic skills. The first, third and fourth points will be discussed in this chapter. Clinical assessment, will be discussed in the chapters on specific problems.

## Rapport

The first priority is to establish rapport with the client, so as to maximize cooperation and motivation. The therapeutic relationship in modern hypnotherapy is one that involves collaboration between therapist and client. Araoz (1982, 1985) has described the TEAM approach in hypnotherapy, which emphasizes the development of *Trust* and positive *Expectations* and *Attitudes* about hypnosis and the utilization of the client's *Motivation*. Rapport can be defined as the development of this TEAM approach.

Some clients come to therapy highly motivated, already possessing positive attitudes and expectations about hypnosis. The development of rapport is generally easy to achieve with these clients. Many others, however, come with fears, negative attitudes, and misconceptions about hypnosis, or they are ambivalent about therapy and the possibility of changing. The therapist needs to take special care in establishing rapport with these clients.

The establishment of rapport can be accomplished in different ways, depending upon the client. With some clients rapport is most effectively established when the therapist shows warmth, caring, and empathy. Other clients are more likely to develop trust on the basis of the prestige, expertise, and authority of the therapist, rather than on the therapist's ability to show concern and understanding. Determining what is important to a given client and then utilizing it effectively depends on the hypnotist's ability to be a good listener and observer. Rapport is often best established through *pacing* and *joining* the client.

Joining occurs when the hypnotist is flexible in her or his style of relating and "speaks the client's language" by acting informal if the client is informal but acting more like an authority figure if the client is more formal. Joining also occurs when the therapist demonstrates willingness to work with the client. Pacing occurs when the therapist's verbalizations match the behavior and experiences of the client. Pacing is also accomplished by giving open-ended suggestions (to be discussed later) that involve generalization and ambiguity and provide the client with several ways of responding. This increases the likelihood that the therapist's suggestions are consistent with the internal experience of the client.

Another method of establishing rapport, which is related to the concepts of pacing and joining, is to tailor the treatment to the expectations of the client. Treatment is more effective when the therapist matches the treatment methods to the client's expectations and requests. Lazarus (1973) conducted a study that illustrates this point. Clients who requested hypnosis were assigned to a treatment labeled either *relaxation* or *hypnosis*. Although the treatments were actually the same for both groups, the clients who received "hypnosis," as they had requested, showed greater improvement than the group who received "relaxation." Based on such findings, as well as clinical experience, we would recommend that, whenever possible, you honor your client's requests. Find out what they expect hypnosis to be like and what methods will work. Within reason, match your suggestions, induction methods, and explanations of their problems to their own interpretations and expectations.

There are, however, limits to how far a therapist can go in utilizing the expectations of clients. If the client's expectations are obviously unrealistic, such as expecting easy, magical, instantaneous cures from hypnosis for difficult problems like obesity, then it would be better to correct such misconceptions. Sometimes the therapist can take a position that is somewhere between the client's expectations and those of the therapist. For example, a client seeking instant results for a long-standing weight problem can be told

> Yes, hypnosis can produce rapid results. It often produces much more rapid results in weight control than many other types of therapy. But it isn't magic. It still requires some effort on your part. So there will be some things that I will be asking you to do, such as practicing self-hypnosis. We will have to work as a team.

We find that joining the client, as demonstrated in this example, is more effective in getting clients to cooperate than simply labeling their expectations *misconceptions*. The concept of pacing and leading is applicable here. First, the therapist finds some areas of agreement. "Yes, hypnosis can produce rapid results," and then the therapist leads "but it isn't magic. It still requires some effort on your part. . . ."

There is some debate as to whether or not rapport is necessary for a subject to experience hypnosis (Clarke & Jackson, 1983; Young, 1927). One might think that, if an individual can learn self-hypnosis from reading a book, then rapport with a hypnotist is unnecessary. If we define rapport as the establishment of trust, positive attitudes and expectations about hypnosis, and motivation toward achieving therapeutic goals, then authors are certainly capable of inducing these feelings about hypnosis in readers. Rapport might also be involved when individuals learn hypnosis from tape recordings and when participating in experimental investigations. Prestige suggestion could be operating in these situations. Many individuals automatically trust anything that is either published or under the auspices of a university.

On the other hand, the necessity of rapport in self-hypnosis is debatable when we consider examples of individuals such as Erickson, who discovered the phenomena of self-hypnosis without the benefit of a hypnotist or a self-hypnosis manual. It could be argued that in self-hypnosis the rapport is with oneself (Salter, 1941). Possibly through the process of trial and error, certain individuals have spontaneous experiences that promote positive expectations and trust in their own cognitive and imaginative skills and abilities. Erickson's earliest experiences with autohypnosis seem to have given him positive expectations and trust in his own ability to overcome his physical handicap and to have motivated him to persist in these efforts.

In practice, the concept of rapport seems clinically very meaningful. Although rapport might not be necessary for an individual to experience hypnosis, it is probably the case that rapport facilitates therapeutic effectiveness. For some clients it seems crucial. Many of them report that they could not work with a previous therapist because they did not trust him or her, or did not feel understood by the therapist, or felt that they were just not on the same "wavelength." Probably one of the reasons why Ericksonian methods are successful with difficult, resistant clients is because many of Erickson's techniques are strategies for establishing rapport. Particularly noteworthy are Erickson's numerous techniques for joining the client and utilizing the client's individual frames of reference (to be discussed later).

## Clarification of Misconceptions

There are several common misconceptions about hypnosis. After rapport is established, the therapist uses the following information to educate and reassure the client about these misconceptions:

*Myth 1: Hypnosis is sleep.* Hypnosis was once thought to be a state similar to sleep. In fact, the word *hypnosis* comes from the Greek word for sleep. Many hypnotists still suggest sleep, or mention sleep, as part of the hypnotic induction procedure. The association that has developed between sleep and hypnosis is unfortunate. People often expect, or fear, that they will be unconscious during hypnosis. Hypnosis is not sleep, however, but is more like a state of highly concentrated attention on one thing to the exclusion of other things. Hypnotic suggestion can be used to produce alertness and concentration as well as relaxation and drowsiness. Even when trance is induced through suggestions of sleepiness and drowsiness, one does not experience a sleeplike state. Experiments in which physiological responses are measured show that subjects who report experiencing trance usually show signs of relaxed wakefulness, not sleep (see Weitzenhoffer, 1963). To avoid reinforcing the misconception that hypnosis is sleep, we recommend suggesting relaxation, not sleepiness, during hypnotic induction.

*Myth 2: One might not wake up from hypnosis.* Because hypnosis is not sleep, one does not have to worry about waking up. Hypnosis usually involves a relaxed or drowsy feeling, although an alert, energized state can also be produced, depending on the type of suggestions given. The suggestion to "be alert" and open the eyes is all that is needed to terminate a hypnotic experience.

A person can inadvertently enter normal sleep during hypnosis, in which case he or she would wake up spontaneously. Passing into a normal sleep happens only if a person is very tired or very bored. Falling asleep during hypnosis has no more significance than falling asleep while watching television.

*Myth 3: Hypnosis can be used to induce individuals to perform antisocial acts.* Research studies have purportedly demonstrated that hypnosis is capable of inducing individuals to engage in dangerous and antisocial behavior. However, in experiments where appropriate control groups were employed, it was found that as many nonhypnotized subjects as hypnotized subjects complied with instructions to perform acts that gave the appearance of being harmful to oneself or to others. Orne and Evans (1965) have explained the compliance of both the hypnotized and nonhypnotized subjects as due to their assumption that proper precautions are taken in scientific studies to guarantee that no one gets harmed. In their study, Orne and Evans did discover, through postexperimental inquiries, that most of the subjects did in fact believe the situation was safe. Therefore it is probably impossible to do a definitive study that could either prove or disprove the ability of hypnosis to induce people to engage in antisocial behavior that they would not do without hypnosis. For a recent review and discussion of the research literature on the antisocial uses of hypnosis see Golden (1986a).

It would not be practical to go into all the details of the literature with your clients. Most hypnotherapists simply tell their clients that hypnosis cannot be used to make them do things against their will. Although oversimplified, this brief explanation is useful in reassuring the client.

A related client concern is that clinical hypnosis might increase one's susceptibility to the influence of an unethical hypnotist. Watkins (1951) has reported that some subjects cannot resist hypnotic induction, especially if they have previously been hypnotized. On the other hand, Young (1927) found that training in self-hypnosis enhanced subjects' ability to resist hypnotic suggestions. Similarly, Araoz (1981, 1982, 1985) has discussed how training in positive self-hypnosis can be used in overcoming one's negative self-hypnosis, that is the uncritical acceptance of one's negative suggestions. Throughout the chapters of this volume we describe examples of how clients can learn to identify their own negative suggestions and to replace them with more positive ones. We maintain that self-control approaches to hypnosis, as described in this volume, can be employed in helping individuals resist negative suggestions, regardless of whether the suggestions are hypnotic or nonhypnotic or are self-suggestions or suggestions from another person.

*Myth 4: Hypnosis weakens the mind.* Just the opposite is true. As pointed out above, training in self-hypnosis can help an individual develop greater self-control and increase resistance to negative influences. In addition, hypnotic procedures can be used to cope with depression, help one break bad habits, overcome fears and phobias, and handle other maladaptive emotions and behaviors.

*Myth 5: Only gullible people respond to hypnosis.* This belief is also untrue. Researchers have failed to find any relationship between receptivity to hypnotic procedures and negative personality traits such as gullibility, dependency, and submissiveness (see Hilgard, 1968). The only ability that is consistently related to hypnotic responsiveness is the ability to become deeply absorbed in activities such as reading novels, watching movies, and role playing that involve the use of one's imagination (Spanos & Barber, 1974).

*Myth 6: Only unintelligent people respond to hypnosis.* Research tends to support the opposite. There is a slight positive correlation between high scores on intelligence tests and hypnotizability (see Weizenhoffer, 1963). The reason that people with severe mental retardation do not respond to hypnotic procedures is because hypnosis requires the ability to concentrate.

*Myth 7: Only emotionally disturbed people respond to hypnosis.* This belief is false. Almost everyone can learn to use and benefit from hypnotic techniques. However, people who are very disturbed, such as those in psychotic states, are usually too disorganized and too distracted to use hypnotic procedures.

## Hypnotic Skills Training

Many hypnotists test their clients for hypnotic susceptibility in order to determine whether they are good candidates for hypnotherapy. Usually the assumption made by these therapists is that hypnotizability is a stable trait that cannot be modified. Although we see the validity of susceptibility testing in scientific studies of hypnosis, our own preference, as clinicians, is to teach clients how to respond to hypnotic suggestions, as opposed to testing them for hypnotic susceptibility. As mentioned in chapter 1, hypnotic skills training has been found to be effective in increasing hypnotic responsiveness.

Almost all of the traditional hypnotic susceptibility tests can be modified for hypnotic skills training. However, instead of being presented as tests, they are presented as exercises that provide clients with practice in developing hypnotic skills. Self-control is emphasized, and clients have experiences similar to self-hypnosis prior to experiencing heterohypnosis. Under these circumstances clients are more likely to develop realistic than magical expectations about hypnosis. They see that hypnosis requires their cooperation and participation and that it is under their control. As a result of skills training, they are more likely to develop an internal locus of control and attribute success to themselves rather than to the hypnotist or the "powers of hypnosis." Research (see, for example, Davison, Tsujimoto, & Glaros, 1973) has found that internal attributions for change are more likely to lead to longer lasting therapeutic results than external attributions for change.

In our clinical experience, skills training is more effective in establishing therapeutic rapport than the traditional method of testing for hypnotic susceptibility. When tested, clients might feel pressured or challenged, and, if they respond poorly to the testing, they can feel defeated. A hypnotist employing susceptibility testing might categorize an initially unresponsive individual as a poor hypnotic subject and, therefore, unsuitable for hypnotherapy. We have found that almost all individuals can learn to become adequate subjects with skills training, although they might not be able to experience all hypnotic phenomena. We have therefore succeeded with a wider group of individuals than would have been predicted by susceptibility tests alone.

## A Transcript for Hypnotic Skills Training

The following is a transcript of the hypnotic skills training procedure that one of the authors has used (Golden, 1982) –

In order for you to learn to respond to complex suggestions that involve changes in your feelings and behaviors, it is important that you first learn to respond to simple suggestions. Therefore we are going to go through a series of exercises that are designed to help you learn how to respond to simple hypnotic suggestions.

Hypnosis is not magical, nor is it something that happens to you. It requires your cooperation and participation. Hypnosis is a skill. Therefore, everyone can learn to respond and with practice you can get better at it.

The skill is in being able to think and imagine along with a suggestion. Hypnosis involves concentrating on thoughts and images that are consistent with the goals of a suggestion. For example, if your goal is relaxation, imagining a pleasant fantasy such as a country, mountain or beach scene would help you to become relaxed. Likewise, you can also create relaxation with your thoughts or what can be called self-suggestions. In the case of relaxation, you could give yourself suggestions such as 'My whole body is beginning to relax. My arms and legs are relaxing . . . . beginning to relax more and more. The relaxation is spreading.' Using pain control as another example, if you wanted to create anesthesia you would use thoughts and fantasies that would produce numbness. You could imagine that you were receiving an injection of Novocain and suggest to yourself 'My hand is becoming numb, I'm feeling less and less sensation. I'm starting to feel a rubbery feeling.' You would continue the imaging and repeat these suggestions until you got the desired effect.

Not only is it important to concentrate on the thoughts and fantasies that will produce the desired result, but it is also important to block out negative thoughts and fantasies that might interfere with your ability to respond to suggestion. If a person who is attempting to create a feeling of numbness focuses on thoughts that are incompatible with anesthesia (such as concentrating on the pain and thinking 'this will never work; I really didn't receive an injection of Novocain', he or she will not obtain the desired results. There are several techniques you can use to block out these negative thoughts.

*Focusing.* Simply focusing your attention and concentration on thoughts and fantasies that are consistent with your goals will usually be sufficient to obtain a successful response to suggestion. This method allows you to distract your attention from negative thoughts that would otherwise interfere with your concentration.

*Thought stopping.* There are several thought-stopping techniques. *First,* think to yourself the word 'Stop' whenever negative thoughts intrude into your consciousness. *Second,* after thinking the word 'stop,' focus again on the thoughts and fantasies that are related to your goal. Each time a negative thought pops into your mind repeat the procedure. Some people find thought stoppage to be most effective when they imagine a traffic stop sign while thinking the word 'Stop!'

*Letting go of negative thoughts and fantasies.* Some people are able to 'let go' of negative thoughts and do not need to use thought stoppage. Letting go refers to letting a thought pass through your mind instead of holding onto it and dwelling upon it. Occasionally, we all have negative and bizarre thoughts. If we are not alarmed by the presence of these thoughts and fantasies and hence do not focus on them, our stream of consciousness will eventually flow to other thoughts. So if negative thoughts intrude, just let them pass and return to the thoughts and fantasies that will produce the desired results.

Now you are ready to apply these strategies to several exercises so that you can discover which techniques work for you. You do not have to respond to all of the suggestions in these exercises in order to be a good hypnotic subject. As long as you are able to respond in some way to some suggestions, you will be capable of experiencing hypnosis.

*Exercise 1: Hand heaviness.* The goal of the hand heaviness exercise is to create a feeling of heaviness in your arm. Before you begin, think of something that would be so heavy that you would eventually be forced to put it down. Make use of relevant experiences from your life. Some images that others have found helpful include (a) holding a shopping bag full of heavy books or groceries, (b) lifting a barbell weight, (c) trying to lift a piece of furniture, (d) holding a bowling ball, and (e) holding a huge book, like a dictionary, in the palm of your hand. You want to imagine holding something heavy which, if real, would make your arm tired and cause you to lower it.

Once you have selected your fantasy for producing hand heaviness, sit back in your chair and close your eyes. Most people can image better with their eyes closed. Hold both arms out in front of you, palms up. Keep your arms straight and parallel to one another. Imagine that you are supporting something very heavy with your dominant hand and arm.

Whatever you choose as your fantasy for heaviness, use as many of your senses as possible to imagine it. See it, its shape, its color, its size. Feel it. Recall the feeling of heaviness you experienced when you actually held or lifted the object.

In addition to using imagery, give yourself suggestions such as 'my arm is feeling heavy, the muscles are getting tired, fatigued. I feel the strain in the muscles. The _____ is so heavy that I can't keep my arm up. I feel the weight pulling my arm down, down.' Use your own words to suggest heaviness and lowering of the arm. It is most important that you work with the suggestions by imagining an appropriate fantasy and thinking the appropriate thoughts. Block out any thoughts that are incompatible with the suggestions. Use focusing, thought stoppage, or the letting-go technique on any negative, competing thoughts. Imagine your arm getting so tired that it begins to drop lower and lower, until you can no longer keep the arm up, and you let it drop.

*Exercise 2: Hand levitation.* This exercise is a little more difficult and requires more concentration and involvement than the preceding one. Think of something that would be consistent with developing a feeling of lightness in one hand. Some common images are (a) a large helium balloon under the palm of your hand; (b) several helium balloons tied around your wrist; (c) your hand is a balloon being pumped up with helium; (d) your hand is a piece of metal being drawn upward by the magnetic force of your head, which is a huge electromagnet; and (e) your arm is being lifted by a series of ropes and pulleys that are being manipulated by you or someone else. Feel free to use your imagination in creating your own fantasies and suggestions. Since the goal is hand levitation, use strategies that result in such strong feelings of lightness that your hand and arm lift up.

When you are ready to begin, close your eyes, and extend your arms straight out in front of you. Use as many senses as possible to imagine your fantasy. If you are using a balloon image, picture its shape, size and color. Feel its texture and buoyancy. Recall how balloons have felt to you in the past.

In order to make one of your hands feel lighter than the other, give yourself suggestions of lightness, such as, 'I feel the lightness in the palm of my hand and throughout my arm. That arm is feeling lighter than the other. I feel slight movement in my fingers. I feel my hand lifting. The arm is lifting higher and higher, lifting up. . . .' Create your own suggestions in your own words. Imagine the balloon lifting up, rising into the air, and finally moving upward toward your face. Repeat the suggestions as many times as needed in order to create feelings of lightness and hand levitation. Give yourself time to respond. Remember to block out any intrusive thoughts that would interfere with the goals of the exercise.

*Exercise 3: Chevreul's pendulum.* Chevreul's pendulum can be constructed by tying a string seven to eight inches long to a finger ring, a washer, or some other weight. Hold the string between the index finger and thumb. Extend your arm out in front of you so that the elbow does not rest against your body or anything else. Stare at the pendulum and imagine it moving clockwise, or back and forth. Wait long enough for the pendulum to move in the imagined direction. Then, imagine the pendulum changing direction and wait for it to actually change direction.

The movement of the pendulum, like the movement on a ouija board, occurs for a simple reason. There is nothing magical about either one. They do not predict the future nor do they have anything to do with extrasensory perception as some people claim. The activity of the pendulum and the ouija board is the result of tiny movements in your fingers, hand and arm. Although unnoticeable to you, these movements are consistent with the imagined movements. This is an example of your thinking affecting your behavior.

*Exercise 4: Arm catalepsy.* The arm catalepsy exercise provides you with another opportunity to practice self-hypnotic skills. The goal of this exercise is to temporarily make your arm stiff and rigid. Think of something that would be consistent with your arm becoming rigid and immobile. Some people imagine their arm in a cast or a splint. Others imagine that their arms are bars of steel or are made of wood. Use your imagination and feel free to create your own fantasy.

First, make a tight fist and hold your arm out straight, stiff and rigid. Close your eyes and imagine your fantasy. Block out any interfering thoughts. While you continue to fantasize that your arm is immobile, and you tell yourself that it is immobile and cannot be bent, try to bend it. As long as you are absorbed in fantasies and thoughts consistent with arm rigidity, you will have difficulty bending your arm. Once you stop imagining your arm as rigid, and you tell yourself you can bend it, you will in fact be able to move your arm easily.

## Hypnotic Induction

There are a number of standardized hypnotic induction procedures. One way to select a hypnotic induction for a given client is to experiment, trying several different standard hypnotic induction procedures, and to discover, through trial and error, which one(s) the client responds to best. There are wide differences in how clients respond to the various induction procedures. Some are most responsive to a hand-levitation technique, whereas others respond better to an eye-fixation or relaxation method. The problem with selecting an induction procedure on the basis of trial and error is that the therapist might begin with one or more of the wrong methods for a particular client. Negative expectations are then likely to develop. The client could lose confidence in either his or her ability to be hypnotized or the therapist's ability to hypnotize. It is for this reason that failure experiences in hypnosis are to be avoided whenever possible.

Several clinical strategies are available to aid the therapist in selecting an induction procedure that is likely to be effective. One way of lessening the impact of a failure experience resulting from trial and error is to inform clients in advance that there are a number of different hypnotic induction procedures. They will respond to some of these but probably not to all of them, and some experimentation will be needed to determine which ones they will respond to best. Furthermore, by demonstrating skill in employing several different methods of hypnotic induction, a therapist can still maintain the client's confidence even if some initial difficulty is encountered in selecting an effective induction procedure. Therefore, it is important to be familiar with several hypnotic induction procedures and not rely on a favorite one only.

*Utilizing expectations and preferences.* Earlier in the chapter we discussed the utilization of expectations in the establishment of rapport. The client's expectations and preferences can also be used in selecting a hypnotic induction procedure. The first thing to consider is any previous experiences the client might have had with hypnosis. Hypnotic induction is easiest with clients who have already experienced hypnosis, so long as the right procedure is used. Usually a good rule of thumb is that whatever procedure worked before will work again. The exception is the client who successfully responded to a prior hypnosis despite some negative feelings about the procedure. Therefore, question the client about all previous experiences with altered states of consciousness including hypnosis, meditation, and relaxation. Find out what the client liked and disliked and tailor your method to the client's preferences. Another way of utilizing the client's preferences is to describe various hypnotic induction procedures such as eye fixation, hand levitation, hand heaviness, and relaxation and have the client select the one he or she prefers.

*Utilizing the client's responses to hypnotic skills training.* Because hypnotic skills training enhances hypnotic responsiveness in general, it usually increases a client's response to a number of hypnotic induction procedures. In addition, hypnotic skills training exercises can be employed as diagnostic indicators of what types of induction procedures are likely to be effective with a given client. Hypnotic skills training exercises are like hypnotic susceptibility tests in that they provide information about how a given client responds to different types of suggestions such as those for hand levitation, hand heaviness, and arm catalepsy. However, unlike tests, they are presented in a very nonchallenging and nonthreatening manner. It is not immediately obvious to clients that their responses are being evaluated.

There are individual differences in how clients respond to the various exercises in the hypnotic skills training program. Many clients find it easiest to respond to hand heaviness and lowering. However, some clients find it is easier to respond to suggestions for hand levitation or arm catalepsy. Others are more responsive to Chevreul's pendulum. These individual differences are exactly what we look for in determining what type of induction procedure might be most appropriate for a given client. If a client is very responsive to suggestions of lightness, we would recommend employing hand levitation for inducing hypnosis. If, however, a client is more responsive to suggestions for heaviness, we would recommend inducing hypnosis via eye fixation,

HMA-C

through hand heaviness and lowering or through both. Arm catalepsy can also be used as an induction procedure. In fact, any suggestion that a client responded to can be used as a hypnotic induction procedure.

Once a procedure is selected on the basis of a client's responses to the hypnotic skills training exercises, hypnotic induction is fairly easy and straightforward. The therapist simply elicits the client's cooperation in inducing hypnosis. The client is told "now let's do another exercise," and the therapist proceeds with instruction, such as "I want you once again to imagine that you have helium balloons attached to your fingers." Once the client responds, the therapist continues with other suggestions such as those for relaxation and deepening, (to be described later).

Usually it is better not to announce "and now I will hypnotize you," because many clients get anxious or defensive upon hearing such a statement. If they perceive it as simply another exercise, like the others prior to it, they relax more easily. So far, none of our clients have complained that we did not warn them that we were going to hypnotize them. Of course this procedure is to be used only with clients who have requested and expect hypnosis.

*Ericksonian techniques.* In Erickson's approach to hypnosis, hypnotic induction is achieved through utilization of the client's own personal associations and natural response tendencies, instead of relying on standardized hypnotic induction procedures. Erickson emphasized the importance of giving suggestions in a permissive, flexible manner that allows the client to respond in his or her own unique way. The therapist joins the client and utilizes whatever responses the client presents. This is accomplished through pacing. As noted, pacing occurs when the suggestions of the hypnotist match, or describe, the client's observable behavior, nonobservable experiences, or both. When the hypnotist's suggestions match the client's already occurring behavior and experience, the client becomes more responsive to subsequent suggestions. The hypnotist can then lead and give more direct suggestions.

Pacing depends on the therapist's ability to be an astute observer and notice small changes in the client's ongoing behavior such as posture and breathing pattern. Suggestions are timed so that they are accurate descriptions of behavior; for example suggesting that the client breathe in as he or she inhales and breathe out as he or she exhales. At first the therapist is careful to speak at a rate and rhythm that is in synchrony with the client's breathing pattern. Leading occurs as the therapist gradually slows down his or her rate of speech and suggests "breathe in" and "breathe out" more slowly. Usually the client's breathing also begins to slow down. Another example of pacing is to suggest to the client who is shifting to a more comfortable position "and as you sink more deeply in the chair. . . ."

Leading then occurs when the therapist adds ". . . you can become more comfortable and start to relax all over."

Another type of pacing occurs when the hypnotist gives suggestions that accurately reflect the client's private experience. This is possible through the use of indirect suggestions. For a more detailed exposition of Erickson's work, the reader is advised to consult Bandler and Grinder (1975); Erickson & Rossi (1979); Erickson, Rossi, and Rossi (1976); and Rossi (1980). Several illustrative examples of indirect suggestion are offered next.

1. *Open-ended suggestions*. Open-ended suggestions are like the ambiguous stimulus materials employed in projective tests, in that they provide opportunities for clients to project their own unique assocations and meanings into them. Because they allow the individual a great deal of freedom in responding to the suggestions, the individual almost certainly responds in some way. Several examples of open-ended suggestions are

1. As you relax, you may be aware of other sensations.
2. You may be aware of some changes during the week.
3. Just be aware of whatever you experience as you stare at that spot.

2. *Truisms*. Many anxious clients try too hard when given direct suggestions. They become anxious and, thus, less responsive when they believe they are expected to respond in a particular manner. Other clients rebel whenever they are directed. The advantage of indirect suggestions is their subtlety. Clients are less likely to develop specific expectations or experience pressure to respond when suggestions are presented in an indirect manner. Thus indirect suggestions reduce anxiety and resistance.

Truisms are statements of fact that cannot be denied. They are indirect suggestions because the client is not asked to respond in any particular manner. A truism only states that it is possible to have certain types of experiences. Therefore, if the client does not respond, no failure is involved, because no direct command was given. Some examples of truisms include the following suggestions:

1. When people stare at a fixed point for a prolonged period of time, usually their eyes get heavy and tired.
2. People can usually relax more easily with their eyes closed.
3. Many people find it relaxing to imagine a peaceful, pleasant scene.

3. *Conversational postulates*. Conversational postulates are indirect suggestions that, like truisms, suggest possibilities without commanding the individual to do or experience anything. Conversational postulates usually begin with "You can" or ask "Can you?" or "Is it possible for you to?"

experience a particular feeling or sensation. If a client fails to respond to a conversational postulate, any negative impact is minimized because no response has been required.

Conversational postulates are very effective suggestions. Erickson has described hypnotic induction procedures for eye fixation and hand levitation in which every suggestion is a question, for example;

1. Can you feel comfortable resting your hands gently on your thighs? (as therapist demonstrates). That's right, without letting them touch each other.
2. Can you let those hands rest ever so lightly so that the fingertips just barely touch your thighs?
3. That's right. As they rest ever so lightly, do you notice how they tend to lift up a bit all by themselves with each breath you take?
4. Do they begin to lift even more lightly and easily by themselves as the rest of your body relaxes more and more?
5. As that goes on, does one hand or the other or maybe both continue lifting even more?
6. And does that hand stay up and continue lifting higher and higher, bit by bit, all by itself? Does the other hand want to catch up with it, or will the other hand relax in your lap?
7. That's right. And does that hand continue lifting with these slight little jerking movements or does the lifting get smoother and smoother as the hand continues upward toward your face?
8. Does it move more quickly or slowly as it approaches your face with deepening comfort? Does it need to pause a bit before it finally touches your face so you'll know you are going into a trance?
9. And will your body automatically take a deeper breath when that hand touches your face as you really relax and experience yourself going deeper? (Erickson & Rossi, 1979, pp. 30–31).

Bandler and Grinder (1975) provided the following guidelines for constructing conversational postulates:

1. Identify a suggestion you want to give, such as eye fixation.
2. Form a command out of the suggestions, such as "Focus your eyes on that spot."
3. Rephrase the command into a possibility, such as "You can focus your eyes on that spot."
4. To construct the question-type of conversational postulate, form a yes/no question out of the command, such as "Can you focus your eyes on that spot?"

4. *Suggestions involving multiple tasks and alternative ways of responding.* According to Erickson, suggestions that involve multiple tasks reduce resistance and increase receptivity as a result of distraction or confusion. Also, when there are several alternative ways of responding, there is greater freedom of choice and less resistance. Furthermore, when alternatives exist, there is a greater probability that the individual will be able to respond to at

least one of the choices. One of Erickson's induction procedures that covers all of the possible ways of responding to hand levitation is the following:

> Shortly your right hand,, or it may be your left hand, will begin to lift up, or it may press down, or it may not move at all, but we will wait to see just what happens. Maybe the thumb will be first, or you may feel something happening to your little finger, but the really important thing is not whether your hand lifts up or presses down or just remains still; rather it is your ability to sense fully whatever feeling may develop in your hand. (Erickson, et al. 1976, p. 78).

Applying Ericksonian principles, one of the authors (W. G.) has found that an eye-fixation induction procedure is more effective when it involves multiple tasks and allows clients alternate ways of responding. Eye closure occurs more rapidly when it is not overemphasized and if the client is given choices of how he or she can respond to the eye fixation. The hypnotist begins with eye fixation and gives some suggestions about eye closure but then shifts to suggestions of relaxation, changes in breathing, and so forth, for example;

> You can pick a spot, any spot will do, and keep on staring at it. If your eyes should wander, just go back to the same spot. Just keep on staring at it until your eyes become tired of it. Then you can let your eyes close and enter a peaceful relaxed state. While you stare at that spot, you may notice some interesting phenomena. Some people experience a blurring of their vision, whereas for others the spot moves, pulsates, or disappears. Some people see a halo or aura around the spot. Others just experience heaviness in their eyelids. The really important thing is for you to notice whatever it is that you experience and to enjoy it. . . .
>
> Now, let your breathing slow down. Take a deep breath and exaggerate your breathing as you inhale slightly. As you exhale, begin to let go of some of the tension in your body, letting your body sink into the chair. Starting to let go of tension, letting it drain out.
>
> Letting your breathing slow down to a more comfortable, relaxed pace. Breathing in slowly and breathing out slowly. Slow, deep, rhythmic breathing. Each and every time you exhale, you can let go of a little bit more tension. Let your body sink into the chair and into an even more relaxed position. Feel your entire body beginning to relax. Feel the relaxation beginning in your arms and legs. Feel your arms and legs become loose, limp, and relaxed . . . just as if you were like a rag doll. Let your arms hang comfortably. Let your shoulders hang loose and limp. Allow your back to go limp. Don't hold yourself together. Instead, let the chair support your body. Let yourself sink into the chair into a more comfortable state.
>
> Let go of any tension in your jaws. Let your jaws hang slack, teeth and lips slightly parted. Feel the relaxation spreading over the surface of your face. Feel your facial muscles becoming smooth and soft. Feel your neck muscles relaxing. Feel your back becoming more relaxed, and feel the relaxation spreading to your stomach and chest muscles. Your arms and legs relax even further, becoming even more loose and limp. Feel the relaxation permeating your body. Become aware of any other pleasant sensations that accompany the relaxation, whether they be changes in your body weight or changes in your body temperature. All these are signs that the relaxation is progressing.

Just continue your slow, deep breathing, feeling yourself drift into even deeper relaxation.

## Standard Hypnotic Induction Procedures

The main thrust of this chapter so far has been to provide readers with a number of strategies for inducing hypnosis, rather than merely presenting transcripts of standardized hypnotic induction procedures. Nevertheless, transcripts of hypnotic induction procedures can be effective with many clients, especially when combined with the guidelines offered in this chapter. We maintain that better results are obtained by an approach that emphasizes strategies of hypnosis such as hypnotic skills training and Erickson's indirect suggestions than by one that relies exclusively on the memorization or reading of standard induction procedures.

However, standard induction procedures do provide the novice hypnotist with examples of hypnotic induction procedures and a comfortable way to begin practicing hypnosis. In addition, they can be effective with highly responsive or motivated people and individuals who have learned to respond to hypnotic suggestions as a result of hypnotic skills training. Furthermore, standard inductions can be modified to incorporate Ericksonian communication devices. Several examples, such as the hand-levitation and eye-fixation induction procedures that were just described, incorporate Ericksonian principles. Another hand-levitation and alert-hypnosis induction can be found in the chapter on depression. Several other hypnotic induction procedures will now be presented. The reader interested in additional induction procedures is referred to Crasilneck and Hall (1985) and Kroger and Fezler (1976). The reader is also referred to the chapter on self-hypnosis in this book for transcripts that clients can use for self-hypnosis.

*The relaxation method.* Relaxation procedures can be used alone or in combination with other hypnotic induction procedures, as with the eye-fixation method described earlier. Relaxation procedures are also appropriate as deepening techniques (to be discussed shortly). Deep breathing; suggestions of relaxation, warmth, heaviness or lightness; and pleasant imagery such as a beach or country scene can all be employed for inducing relaxation. We would recommend against suggesting heaviness to certain clients such as those who wish to lose weight. Whenever possible, involve the client in the selection of relaxation techniques. It can be helpful to ask him or her to construct an image that is personally pleasant rather than constructing one for the client or using some standardized image. This involves the client in the process of hypnosis. The following exercise can be modified accordingly:

You can close your eyes and find a comfortable relaxed position. Let your body go limp and let yourself sink into the chair.

Let your breathing start to slow down, so that you are breathing slowly and deeply. A comfortable, relaxed breathing pattern, where you are breathing in slowly and breathing out slowly . . . a comfortable rhythmic breathing pattern. . . .

And as you continue to breathe slowly and deeply, your whole body will become relaxed . . . starting with your arms and legs. Feel your arms and legs starting to relax. Arms and legs hanging loose and limp, just as if you were a rag doll. Hands open, fingers apart, wrists loose and limp. Feel the relaxation spreading up and down your arms, all the way up to your shoulders. Just let your shoulders hang comfortably. Feel the relaxation spreading.

And your legs, hanging loose and limp. Feel the relaxation spreading all the way down to your toes. Feel your toes and feet relax as you let your toes spread apart. Feel the relaxation in your ankles, calves, knees, and thighs. Both legs becoming more and more relaxed.

Notice that, with each exhalation, you can feel yourself becoming more relaxed. Feel the relaxation spread with each exhalation. Breathing slowly and deeply. And, with each exhalation, feel yourself sinking into the chair more and more, into a deep relaxation.

Feel the relaxation spreading to your back and neck. Just let your back go loose and limp. Feel yourself sinking into the chair even more, so that you are not holding yourself together. You're letting the chair support your body. Letting your neck be supported by the chair. Feeling the relaxation spreading, spreading to your stomach muscles, spreading throughout your body. Let your jaws hang slack, teeth slightly parted and feel the relaxation spreading to your facial muscles, permeating your body. Feeling more and more relaxed. Continuing to breathe slowly and deeply and feeling more and more relaxed.

And to deepen your relaxation, you can imagine your peaceful relaxing scene, the one we discussed before. Imagine it as clearly and as vividly as you can, what it looks like, what you would see if you were there now looking out and enjoying the scenery . . . what you would hear . . . what you would feel . . . what you would smell . . . or taste . . . just keep on imagining the peaceful scene, continuing to breathe slowly and deeply and feeling yourself becoming even more relaxed. Arms and legs, more relaxed. Shoulders hanging comfortably. Back and neck loose and limp. Jaws hanging slack. Facial muscles, smooth and relaxed. Stomach muscles, relaxed. All the muscles of your body relaxed, and your mind feeling calm and peaceful. As you continue to imagine that peaceful, serene scene and continue to breathe slowly and deeply, you become more and more relaxed.

*Eye fixation combined with hand heaviness.* Hold your hand up in front of you above eye level and point your index finger upward. (Demonstrate the position to the client. Make sure that the client's arm is high enough so that his or her eyes are strained by staring at the tip of the finger.)

Keep on staring at that spot until your eyes and arm get so heavy that your arm lowers and your eyes close. Just keep on staring at the tip of your finger. If your eyes should wander, just focus back on the same spot until they become heavy and tired. Notice whatever sensations result from your staring at the same spot. Your vision might become blurry, or begin to double, or start to fade. You might notice that your eyes blink more rapidly. No matter what you experience, keep on staring at the tip of your finger.

Notice that your arm is getting heavy . . . so heavy . . . so heavy that it is getting
tired. . . . Your eyes are getting tired . . . your arm tired and heavy . . .
fatigued . . . you feel the strain in the muscles . . . feel your arm getting so
heavy that you feel like lowering it.

Every time you exhale you notice how there is a tendency for your arm to lower.
And as your arm gets so heavy that it starts to lower, your eyes also start to
close. As your arm moves down, your eyes move down. Lower . . . lower . . .
so heavy . . . down . . . down . . . feel the heaviness in the eyes . . . so heavy
that you just want to close them so that you can enter a peaceful relaxed state.
. . . (Repeat these suggestions until the client's arm is all the way down and the
eyes are closed. If these suggestions fail to produce eye closure, say "Now just
lower your arm all the way, just rest your arm," and, if the client's eyes are still
open, say "and now close your eyes all the way, eyes closed.")

*Chiasson's Method.* Chiasson's (1973) method of hypnotic induction is
useful with resistant clients or those who have difficulty relaxing. Almost
everyone responds, because it is based on the tendency of the fingers to
spread apart when they are firmly held together and for one's arms to move
upward toward the face as one inhales. The opposite tends to occur when one
exhales: There is a tendency for one's arms to sink downward. This
connection between breathing and arm movements has been incorporated
into hand-levitation and hand-lowering induction procedures. These
techniques make use of common, but unnoticed, physical phenomena and
hence can be seen as involving a certain trickiness or manipulation toward
the therapist's wishes. They are not congruent with a self-control model.
However, we recognize that some clients do *not* respond to a self-control
model because of ambivalences or outright resistance. Hence the need for
methods such as these that overcome client resistance and enhance
motivation.

In using Chiasson's method, instruct the client to hold a hand a distance of
one foot in front of his or her face, palm away, with the fingers held firmly
together. Before there is an opportunity for the fingers to spontaneously
spread apart from the strain placed on them from being in this position, the
following is suggested:

Hold up your hand and look at the back of your hand. Hold your hand up close
to your face. Hold it out about 12 in. right in front of you. Close the fingers
tightly together so there are no spaces between them. Hold your hand in that
position.

Now watch the fingers of your hand and notice what happens. Concentrate on
your fingers and notice that, as you concentrate on them, they start to spread
apart. Watch the spaces between your fingers becoming wider. Little by little,
the fingers spread apart more and more. They seem to come alive.

You might also notice that, each time you inhale, your hand moves a little bit
toward your face. With each inhalation it will move closer and closer. It's as if
there were a magnetic force drawing your hand closer and closer to your face.
The magnetic force pulls your hand closer.

If the client's hand continues to move in the suggested direction, continue with similar suggestions that the hand will move toward the client's face. But if the client's hand moves in the opposite direction, start to suggest heaviness, followed by suggestions that the hand will get so heavy as to move downward and the eyes will close. Remember to suggest the downward movement as the client exhales. If the client responds to your suggestions about the hand moving toward his or her face, then continue with the following suggestions:

> As your hand gets closer to your face, you might notice that your eyes are getting heavy. As soon as your hand touches your face, you can take a deep breath and, as you exhale, close your eyes, letting your hand slowly descend into your lap.

Repeat the suggestions and vary the pace so as to match the client's movements and rate of response.

## Deepening Techniques

A number of techniques can be used to deepen hypnosis. Exactly what is being deepened is not clear and is the subject of theoretical controversy. Because this book is intended to be a clinician's treatment manual, we will not discuss this theoretical issue. From the clinical standpoint, most people experience hypnotic depth as increased feelings of relaxation, greater absorption or concentration and narrowing of one's attention, or, in the case of alert hypnosis, increased energy.

We have already described relaxation techniques (deep breathing, pleasant imagery, and suggestions of relaxation) that can be used for the purposes of deepening. Other deepening techniques are described in the self-hypnosis chapter. Induction techniques can also be used interchangeably as deepening techniques. For example, if you employ hand levitation as an induction procedure, you can use relaxation for deepening. On the other hand, if you use relaxation techniques to induce hypnosis, you can use hand levitation as a deepening technique. Now we will describe in detail two commonly used deepening techniques, the stairway image and the counting technique.

*The stairway image.* The client is asked to imagine herself or himself walking down a long stairway and, with each step, going into a deeper state of hypnosis. Some clients prefer elevators or escalators, but be sure not to use one of these as a deepening technique with clients who are afraid of them. Some clients feel more in control if they have the freedom to choose how deep they will go. It can be helpful to discuss with the client the type of deepening technique to be used.

Self-control can be introduced into the imagery by having clients imagine that they control the elevator, increasing or decreasing the depth of the hypnosis at the push of a button or, in the case of the stairway image, going down only as far as they wish. Some clients prefer the elevator to go up to increase their trances, although most clients associate depth with going down. Alter the following procedure in accordance with each client's preferences:

> And now you can go into a deeper state of hypnosis. Imagine yourself walking down a long, long stairway . . . picture each and every step you are taking. Each step you take helps you to enter a deeper state of hypnosis, and you can go as deep as you want by going down as many steps as you choose, down, deeper and deeper, every step, taking you deeper. You're walking down further and further, becoming more and more relaxed with each step.

*Counting technique.* With this deepening procedure the therapist counts from 1 to 10 (or some other count such as from 1 to 20) and suggests that, with each count, the client will experience a deepening of the hypnosis:

> Now I am going to count from 1 to 10. During this count from 1 to 10 you will be able to feel yourself going into a deeper state of hypnosis . . . 1 — the counting helps you to go deeper, 2 — each number brings you to a deeper level, 3 — letting yourself go as deep as you want, 4 — continuing to breathe slowly and deeply, 5 — and with each count, each exhalation, you feel yourself becoming more relaxed, 6 — more and more relaxed, 7 — deeper and deeper, 8 — feeling yourself going even deeper, 9 — deeper, 10 — in a deep, deep state of relaxation, feeling so relaxed all over.

## Utilization of Hypnosis for Therapeutic Purposes

The induction and deepening of hypnosis alone do not usually produce lasting therapeutic results. Hypnosis is only the context in which therapy takes place. During the hypnosis the therapist utilizes various therapeutic interventions, depending on the nature of the client's problems. Therapeutic suggestions and imagery are typically employed. The specific interventions are the subject matter of the chapters describing various clinical problem areas.

## Termination of Hypnosis

A popular method of terminating hypnosis is to count from 1 to 5 or 1 to 10 while giving suggestions that the client is returning to the fully alert, wide-awake state, for example;

> I'm now going to count from 1 to 5. At the count of five you will open your eyes feeling refreshed, alert and wide awake. 1 — beginning to return to the alert state, 2 — feeling wonderful,, 3 — refreshed, 4 — starting to move a little, 5 — starting to open your eyes, moving about, feeling wonderful, relaxed, refreshed, wide awake.

Another method is to give full control to the client and let the client make the transition to the alert state at his or her own pace. No matter which method is used, it is important to allow enough time for this transition. The advantage of the client-controlled method of terminating hypnosis is that it allows individual differences in the amount of time appropriate for a given client:

> Now you will begin, at your own pace, to return to the fully alert, wide-awake state. Feel free to take your time. Go at a pace that is comfortable for you. Take it slowly. Start to move a little, very slowly and at your pace, starting to open your eyes, returning to an alert state, feeling relaxed, refreshed, and wide awake.

## SUMMARY OF THE FIVE STAGES
## OF HYPNOTIC TREATMENT

1. *Preparation of the client for hypnosis.* Establishment of rapport, assessment of the client's problems, clarification of misconceptions, skills training, or susceptibility testing.

2. *Hypnotic induction.*

3. *Deepening techniques.*

4. *Utilization of hypnosis for therapeutic purposes.*

5. *Termination of hypnosis.*

# Chapter 3

# Depression

There are many indications of depression. Although some symptoms, such as crying spells, are recognized by almost everyone, other signs are not as obvious. Depressive symptoms can be divided into the following categories:

1. Emotional symptoms, such as crying spells, dejected mood, and overall sadness. These are what most people think of as depression.
2. Cognitive symptoms, such as excessive self-criticism and low self-evaluation. The individual blames himself or herself for everything and constantly ruminates about personal failures or shortcomings. Beck, Rush, Shaw, and Emery (1979) have described the treatment of this aspect of depression thoroughly and argue that depression results from a negative view of self, the world, and the future.
3. Behavioral symptoms, such as low motivation, avoidance, withdrawal, and low energy. The individual finds it increasingly difficult to accomplish even simple tasks and sometimes remains at home or even in bed.
4. Physical symptoms, such as sleep disturbance, loss of appetite, and loss of interest in sex. The person might sleep most of the time or very little. The person might eat very much or very little. The important point, however, is that the usual pattern of behavior is disrupted.

Although no one client exhibits all or even most of these symptoms, he or she might show more than one. It is important, therefore, to look carefully at exactly which symptoms each client has and to conduct a multifaceted treatment program if necessary.

## BIOCHEMICAL DEPRESSION

Depression can involve disturbances in thought, mood, behavior, and biochemistry. The degree of involvement of each of these factors varies from individual to individual. For one person, biochemical disturbances might be more significant; for another individual, psychological factors might be more significant. Clients with bipolar depression (manic–depressive illness) and many clients with biochemical unipolar depression require medication. Therefore, an assessment of biochemical factors for all clients suffering from depression should be conducted.

If the client is deeply depressed, exhibits any of the physical manifestations of depression, or is suicidal, it is important to refer him or her to a psychiatrist to determine whether medication is needed. Some of the physical manifestations, or vegetative signs as they are usually called by psychiatrists, considered indicative of a biochemical imbalance are early morning awakening, loss of appetite, change in libido, and extreme fatigue. Other symptoms that have been used as signs of a physical basis for depression include agitation, "diurnal" variation in mood, that is, a worsening of symptoms in the morning; increased appetite, impaired concentration, and family history of depression. Other signs of a biochemical imbalance are bipolar depression and severe depression in the absence of a precipitating event. In addition, several biochemical tests (the dexamethasone suppression test and the thyrotropin releasing hormone test) are being used to identify biochemical subgroups of unipolar depression (Gold, Pottash, Extein, & Sweeney, 1981).

## PSYCHOLOGICAL DEPRESSION

### Reactive Depression

There are several types of psychological depression. *Reactive depression* is a commonly used term that refers to depression occurring in response to a loss or disappointment. However, some theorists, such as Ellis (1962), make a distinction between sadness and depression. Sadness is adaptive, because it motivates the individual to do something constructive about the situation. Depression, on the other hand, is maladaptive, because it usually results in withdrawal and immobility. According to Ellis, self-defeating attitudes and beliefs cause one to be depressed, as opposed to just being sad over loss, rejection, failure, or disappointment. For the most part, we are in agreement with this position. We believe that cognitions either directly cause depression or interfere with an individual's ability to overcome it. Beck and his associates have provided compelling evidence that, whether or not cognitions cause depression, cognitive–behavioral strategies are very effective in treating depression, equal to or more effective than antidepressant medication (Beck, Hollon, Young, & Bedrosian, 1985; Blackburn, Bishop, Glen, Whalley, & Christie 1981; Dunn, 1979; Rush, Beck, Kovacs, & Hollon, 1977). Fuller (1981) found that a combination of hypnosis and cognitive restructuring procedures was even more effective than cognitive techniques alone or hypnosis alone in treating depression.

Irrespective of one's theoretical orientation, the first strategy in treating any type of depression (or sadness) is to mobilize the client into constructive action. It is also important and sometimes necessary to help clients modify maladaptive attitudes, beliefs, and cognitive styles. Several patterns of thinking relevant to depression can be identified. They can be classified according to whether they involve self-condemnation, hopelessness, or self-pity.

## Self-Condemnation

Self-condemnation leads to feelings of inadequacy, worthlessness, and guilt. Individuals who feel guilty condemn themselves as "bad" or worthless for having done something wrong. They might not have actually done anything wrong; it could be only their mistaken belief or someone else's opinion. People who suffer from feelings of inadequacy also feel worthless. They condemn themselves as being inadequate or incompetent for making mistakes, having failed at something, or being rejected. In this case it is not the failure or rejection alone that causes the individual to feel depressed; it is also the loss in self-esteem as a result of self-condemnation that causes the person to feel inadequate or worthless.

## Hopelessness

Individuals become depressed when they believe they are helpless and hopeless. These beliefs provide an excellent example of how negative thinking can be hypnoticlike, or what was referred to in earlier chapters as negative self-hypnosis (Araoz, 1981). The belief that one is helpless and hopeless is a very powerful self-fulfilling prophecy. When people believe they are helpless and everything is hopeless, they act in accordance with their beliefs. They act helpless and give up. Once they give up, there is, of course, less chance that things will improve and more reason for them to feel depressed, leading to a maladaptive spiral.

## Self-Pity

Although it is natural and normal to feel sad when one suffers a loss or misfortune, self-pity is maladaptive because it leads to depression. Depression is immobilizing, making it more difficult for the individual to change the situation or find substitute satisfactions.

Self-pity usually stems from *magnification*, a term used by Beck (1976), or *catasrophizing* as Ellis (1962) called it, about one's misfortune.

Catasrophizing and magnification involve preoccupation and exaggeration of the significance of a problem. Depression occurs when one treats a disappointment, loss, or rejection as if it were a catastrophe. Although these events are truly unfortunate and unpleasant, individuals become depressed when they lose perspective and think of them as terrible, unbearable tragedies. These clients are often angry as well as depressed about the unfairness of life and perceive themselves as victims. Clients suffering from self-pity can be identified by phrases such as Why me? and the attitude of "poor me." They become passive and wallow in their self-pity, instead of engaging in constructive action to remedy the situation.

## DIAGNOSIS AND ASSESSMENT OF DEPRESSION

This classification of depression as stemming from biochemical factors or psychological factors such as self-condemnation, hopelessness and helplessness, and self-pity is a clinically useful way of distinguishing different types of depression. Specific interventions can be employed depending on the diagnosis: medication and cognitive–behavioral therapy for those clients exhibiting signs of a biochemical imbalance and a combination of hypnotherapy and cognitive restructuring for clients who exhibit psychological symptoms.

Self-report measures of depression can be used to determine the degree of depression. The authors have found the Beck Depression Inventory (BDI) ( see Beck, et al, 1979) and the Hopelessness Scale (HS) developed by Beck, Weissman, Lester, and Trexler (1974) to be particularly useful in measuring depression. The HS has been found to be better than the BDI at predicting suicide attempts (see Beck, Kovacs, & Weissman, 1975) and seems to be measuring a different type of depression than that measured by the BDI. The BDI is heavily loaded with questions about self-condemnation and self-depreciation, whereas the HS measures what we have distinguished earlier as helplessness and hopelessness. For example, items from the BDI include "I feel I am a complete failure as a person, I feel guilty all of the time, I feel I am being punished, I hate myself, I blame myself for everything bad that happens, I believe that I look ugly." The BDI has only one question tapping hopelessness: "I feel the future is hopeless and that things cannot improve," whereas the HS includes items such as "I might as well give up because there's nothing I can do about making things better for myself. I don't expect to get what I really want. It is very unlikely that I will get any real satisfaction in the future. My future seems dark to me."

In sum, there are different types of psychological depression that result from different types of thinking: (a) cognitions involving self-condemnation and self-depreciation result in the type of depression best measured by the BDI, (b) cognitions about the future and one's ability to alter it result in the type of depression measured by the HS, and (c) cognitions that involve self-pity and do not have a measure as yet.

A given client can have a combination of these types of psychological depression. The advantage, however, of classifying a client's depression into these distinct categories is that it is then possible to construct hypnotic suggestions directed toward the modification of specific attitudes and beliefs causing depression. As will be shown shortly, hypnosis has value as a cognitive-restructuring procedure in addition to providing symptom relief from depression.

Hypnosis can be used to reduce depression in several ways: (a) by motivating and energizing clients who would otherwise be too depressed and lethargic to engage in pleasurable and constructive activity; (b) by reducing phobic anxiety that inhibits clients from pursuing goals, restricts their social interaction, or prevents them from enjoying other satisfactions in life; and (c) as a method of cognitive restructuring whereby maladaptive attitudes, beliefs, and patterns of thinking that contribute to depression are modified.

Despite our enthusiasm about using hypnosis in the treatment of depression, some caution is advised. Because relaxation procedures produce low arousal states, and depression is already a low arousal state, improper use of hypnosis and relaxation techniques can make a client feel more depressed. Nevertheless, those clients who are phobic or who experience a combination of anxiety and depression can derive benefits from relaxation procedures.

Although hypnosis usually entails the induction of a relaxed state, it can also be used to induce an energized state. Alert hypnosis, has application in the area of sports psychology (see Golden, Friedberg, & Richman, 1983) as well as in the treatment of depression. More will be said about alert hypnosis later in the chapter.

For those clients who experience a combination of anxiety and depression, we offer the following strategy. First teach clients to discriminate between depression and anxiety. Many clients at first only know they feel "bad." They have not learned to attach the proper labels to the various affective states they experience. A simple distinction often suffices — "When your body feels all charged up or uptight you are feeling anxiety. If you feel low, have trouble enjoying activities that you used to enjoy, or feel so tired that you don't feel like doing anything, you are probably depressed." Once a client understands this distinction, he or she is advised to employ hypnotic-relaxation procedures when anxious but not when depressed. Instead, when depressed, the client is advised to activate himself or herself by engaging in pleasurable or constructive activity or by using alert hypnosis.

# ALERT HYPNOSIS

Hypnosis is usually thought of as a relaxed or drowsy state. But hypnosis can also create an energetic, activated state. In research done by Hilgard (Banyai & Hilgard, 1976), hypnotic subjects were given suggestions for alertness, after which they increased their performance on a stationary bicycle above their nonhypnotic levels. Hilgard has suggested that long-distance runners who experience a "second wind" might be using some form of alert hypnosis to energize themselves. We have applied alert hypnosis to the treatment of depression as well as to sports psychology. Its application in sports psychology is as a tool for increasing the strength, endurance, and speed of athletes. As mentioned earlier, hypnotic procedures that involve inducing a relaxed state can lower an already low arousal state and intensify depression. In treating depression, alert hypnosis has value as an induction procedure that does not involve deep relaxation. Instead, energizing suggestions and imagery are given to increase the arousal level of depressed clients suffering from chronic fatigability.

We will give a sample of a hand-levitation procedure that can be used as an alert hypnosis induction procedure with depressed clients. If a client is not responsive to suggestions for hand levitation, modify the procedure by instructing the client to simply close his or her eyes and begin the induction with the second paragraph, which contains energizing imagery and suggestions. Some clients do not like or relate to the particular energizing imagery selected here for illustrative purposes. In that case, ask the client to collaborate with you in constructing one that is more appropriate. For example, one client found imagining herself swimming to be more invigorating than imagining herself taking a walk in the woods. Another client found the walk-in-the-woods image to be anxiety-producing. She lived in New York City, and the only woods that she could think of was the local park, where one could be mugged, raped, or killed. In her case, jogging on the beach was used instead.

When inducing alert hypnosis, speak in a lively manner, not in the usual quiet lulling voice that is employed to induce a relaxed state. Remember the goal is to energize the client. Gradually increase the tempo of your voice as you elaborate on the details of what the client would actually experience if he or she were actively engaged in the activity.

> Close your eyes and let each hand rest gently on your legs. Imagine something that would make one of your hands light and buoyant, such as helium balloons attached to the fingers of one of your hands. . . . Be aware of whatever sensations develop in your hand. . . . Notice the difference between your hands. Notice how one hand is starting to feel lighter than the other. . . . Feel the lightness spreading . . . spreading throughout your hand . . . to your arm. . . . Spreading throughout your arm. . . . Your hand is getting lighter. . . .

Getting lighter. . . . Your arm is getting lighter . . . so much lighter than your other hand and arm. . . . Soon it will feel so light that your hand will start to lift. . . . Feeling so light that it feels like lifting, like floating. Light and buoyant, and as your hand and arm become light and buoyant, your whole body starts to feel light and comfortable. . . . As your hand lifts, you feel more and more energetic, alive, feeling pleasant sensations throughout your body. Comfortable, but alert. You can feel positive and confident that you can control your feelings. Just as you can control simple sensations like lightness, you can control other feelings too.

Now imagine that you are taking a pleasant walk in the woods on a nice, warm, spring day. The sky is clear and blue, and the air crisp and clean. The leaves are on the trees, and the flowers are in full bloom. You're aware of their pleasant fragrance. There's a gentle, refreshing breeze that you can feel against your cheeks, although you are also aware of the warmth of the sun that makes you feel quite comfortable. You're walking down a path that takes you into the woods. You can hear the sound of the birds chirping in the trees, and you see chipmunks all full of energy scurrying about. You hear a bubbling brook that is running along the path. It's very invigorating to hear that bubbling sound. You pick up the pace and start to walk a bit more quickly. It feels good. You feel your whole body starting to come alive. You feel a force of energy spreading throughout your body. The energy is spreading all over, to your arms and legs. Each time you inhale, you feel yourself becoming more energized. You feel your heart beating stronger, spreading the energy throughout your body. It feels great to be outside, having nature all around you; breathing clean, fresh air; feeling activated. And this feeling will persist and stay with you for longer and longer periods of time. Whenever you need a lift, all you have to do is think about taking this invigorating walk, imagining what you will see, what you will hear, smell, and feel, and you will begin to feel more energetic, more like doing things, being more active.

# TIME PROJECTION

Depressed individuals typically experience lack of energy and loss of pleasure, and they withdraw from activity. Regardless of whether the lack of activity and pleasure causes depression, as some theorists maintain (Ferster, 1973; Lewinsohn, 1974) or is a result of depression, a vicious circle develops as soon as a depressed individual withdraws from pleasurable and constructive activity. One way of breaking the vicious circle is to encourage clients to act against the depression by increasing their activity. However, depressed individuals often protest that nothing gives them pleasure or that they are too depressed to do anything. An alert-hypnosis induction procedure like the one previously described is capable of energizing many depressed individuals sufficiently so that their activity level increases. A similar method that can, at least temporarily, increase their mood and energy level enough to prompt them into action is Lazarus's (1968) *time-projection* technique.

Time projection is an imagery procedure in which the depressed client is instructed to imagine himself or herself in the future becoming more active, enjoying life, and feeling better as time progresses. When a hypnotic induction is used prior to the time projection, one with energizing suggestions and imagery such as the alert hypnosis procedure described before would be particularly appropriate.

The first step is to ask the client to construct a list of activities and experiences that currently give pleasure or that the client used to enjoy prior to his or her depression. These pleasurable experiences can be very simple things that one often takes for granted, such as a warm bath, a back rub, music (but not sad music), a newspaper or book, and television or a movie (but not a sad one). Other items on the list could include watching a sunset and talking to a friend and physical activities like riding a bicycle, dancing, playing tennis, swimming, taking a walk, eating (within limits) a favorite food, going to museums, and socializing and going to parties.

The time projection may be initiated after a hypnotic induction or may be employed alone as an energizing induction procedure. The client is asked to imagine himself or herself progressively further into the future, engaging in various pleasurable activities. Throughout the imagery, the therapist gives suggestions that the client is enjoying these activities, is feeling better, and will be more inclined to experience them in reality. Tape recordings of the procedure can be made for the client to listen to at home. Or the client can be taught how to employ time projection on her or his own as a self-hypnotic procedure. Or both methods can be used.

Mary, who was severely depressed, found time projection to be particularly helpful. She felt inadequate because, at 35, she was unmarried, unattractive, and felt hopeless about ever getting married. She also believed she would be incapable of enjoying life without marriage. She threatened to commit suicide if she did not find someone by age 36. Her treatment program included antidepressant medication and cognitive therapy. However, neither of these treatments was successful in reducing her depression enough to improve her functioning or to control her suicidal thoughts. She would remain in bed weeping and sometimes angrily scream and hit the walls. Mary requested hypnosis, which she believed was her last resort. The therapist (W. G.) decided that the first intervention should be designed to get her energized and active. At first, Mary insisted that nothing could give her pleasure except being married and having children. However, her history revealed that, when she was much younger, she had enjoyed painting, singing, and playing the guitar by herself, as well as having other people hear her perform. She also enjoyed listening to music, taking trips to the country, dancing, and swimming. An alert-hypnosis induction and time projection were utilized in the following manner:

> Do you remember when you used to go swimming in the country? (Client answers yes.) Do you remember what it felt like? (Client nods.) You can close your eyes and recall a time when you went swimming. Remember standing by

the lake, feeling a cool refreshing breeze against your body, breathing the clean fresh country air. Remember walking into the lake and feeling the cool refreshing water. How you felt a shiver through your body . . . you know that can be very invigorating, and how you dove in and the feeling of the cool fresh water surrounding your body, making your body come alive. . . . Feeling your heart beating, feeling its energy spreading throughout your body as you glide through the water. Each stroke, each kick, feeling it, the power in your body, feeling strong and powerful, feeling all the muscles of your body working and getting stronger. Keep on imagining this and, as soon as you feel some of these sensations, let me know with a head nod. (Client nods.)

And now you can imagine that you are home, and some time this week you are listening to your favorite rock music. You can hear and feel the rhythm of the drums and bass guitar. You find, from time to time, that you get so into the music that you are tapping your toes in rhythm to it.

Now, you're sitting at your easel and beginning to paint. You're feeling 'up,' and your strokes are lively. You're painting some of your favorite scenery and thinking about being there, enjoying it. It's a country scene.

And now you can imagine some time later that week you pick up your guitar. You're playing with your electric guitar. You're getting more and more into playing. You're really letting yourself go and really getting into the beat. You start singing.

And now it's several weeks from now. You're at a party. You brought your guitar because your friend asked you to play it at her party. She knows how well you play. You're a little anxious, but its exciting. You know how that anticipation builds up and how it makes it all the more exciting. You feel your heart beating, and you feel the adrenalin flowing through your body, helping you get ready to perform. And now you're playing in front of the group. It feels good getting all that attention. You're singing, and its a familiar lively tune. People are joining in, singing along with you. You feel proud and appreciate your talent.

Now you've finished performing, and people are coming up to you praising your performance and your ability. You love it, but you're not so surprised. It's always like that. Just as you've experienced in the past, people are gravitating toward you, talking to you about your performance and other things. Several men have approached you and spend time with you. They seem interested. You're feeling good. Feeling more positive about yourself, life, and the future.

And just as you've experienced these feeling now, you can experience them in the future. Whenever you're feeling down or if you have difficulty getting out of bed, just turn on the tape recording of this session. Keep the recorder by your bed, so it won't require much effort to just lean over and turn it on. Feel free to lie in bed listening to your hypnosis tape, becoming more and more energized, feeling positive about your ability to experience joy and feeling more positive about the future. And now you can open your eyes feeling refreshed and wide awake.

Mary reported feeling immediate elevation in mood and energy level. Several such tapes were made, and she was also taught how to induce the energized state on her own, self-hypnotically. She did become more active and started to feel relief from depression. The alert hypnosis and the time projection elevated her mood and energized her enough to mobilize her into action. After reporting some symptomatic relief, she became more receptive to the previously unsuccessful cognitive-restructuring procedures. Actually Mary's response to treatment is not unusual. We have found that, in the treatment of depression, the best results are obtained when the first therapeutic interventions are focused upon getting clients to increase their activity levels. Then, after some symptomatic relief is achieved, cognitive-restructuring procedures are more effective.

Consistent with this viewpoint is research reported by one of the authors that found that treatment for depression was more effective when behavioral techniques involving the use of pleasurable and constructive activity were used prior to cognitive interventions (Kelly, Dowd, & Duffey, 1983).

## COGNITIVE–BEHAVIORAL HYPNOTHERAPY

Once hypnotic energizing techniques are effective in mobilizing the client and creating some pleasurable feelings, cognitive-restructuring techniques can be incorporated into therapeutic hypnosis. Cognitive–behavioral hypnotherapy can be subdivided into two basic steps.

1. *"Uncovering" or identification of self-defeating thoughts attitudes, and beliefs* – Depressed clients are taught how their thoughts operate as a type of *negative self-hypnosis* and are shown how to identify the negative suggestions they give themselves.

2. *Cognitive restructuring* – Clients are taught how to replace negative self-suggestions (self-defeating thoughts) with positive, constructive suggestions.

### Uncovering Techniques

The first step in cognitive–behavioral hypnotherapy is to identify beliefs and patterns of thinking that cause or maintain the client's depression. The following techniques have been useful.

### Self-Monitoring

Depressed clients do not have much difficulty uncovering their maladaptive thoughts. In depression, these negative self-suggestions are in the forefront of consciousness. Earlier, we categorized these negative patterns of thinking as involving self-condemnation, hopelessness, or self-pity. Teaching clients this classification system makes it easier for them to pinpoint their own specific depressive patterns of thinking. Clients are instructed that, whenever they feel depressed, they are to write down whatever it is they are thinking or suggesting to themselves for example, "I'm no good. I'll never be happy. It's hopeless. I might as well give up."

## Evocative Imagery

With or without a prior hypnotic induction, imagery can be used to evoke thoughts, fantasies, and feelings. Imagery heightens awareness and enables clients to identify attitudes, beliefs, and patterns of thinking that they could not pinpoint through their own self-monitoring. In terms of its ability to heighten awareness, evocative imagery is similar to hypnotic age regression. However, wheras age regression is used to provide clients with insight by exploring the remote past, evocative imagery is usually directed toward providing insight about recent and reoccurring events.

An advantage of evocative imagery over self-monitoring is that some depressed clients become overwhelmed when they attempt introspection on their own. For these clients, self-monitoring, at least in the initial stages of treatment, can *increase* depression. Therapists are better able to control the outcome of imagery by controlling the amount of introspection that takes place and being present if a client has an adverse reaction. In addition, clients often feel more secure examining their thoughts and feelings in the presence of a therapist than when they are alone.

Evocative imagery was used with Alice, who was aware of feeling very depressed but was not aware of the reasons for it. She was not suicidal, nor did she report any suicidal thoughts. She did show some biological signs of depression (excessive sleeping and weight gain) but refused medication. Although she had remained depressed since her husband's death 5 years before, her current depression seemed to be only partly due to prolonged grief. Another factor was her lack of assertiveness. Alice typically allowed other people to take advantage of her. For example, at work, where she held a middle-management position, she was having difficulties dealing with subordinates, especially a male employee who intimidated her. Another contributing factor was that, other than going to work, Alice was inactive and did nothing for pleasure.

Alert hypnosis and time projection were employed to energize her and induce her to try some pleasurable activities. Although responsive to these procedures in the office, she complained that she was still too depressed to do anything, even after listening to tape recordings of the procedures at home. After a brief hand-levitation hypnotic induction, Alice was asked to imagine herself in some of the situations at work that she found upsetting. The following dialogue took place between Alice and her therapist (W. G.) after the hand-levitation procedure:

*Therapist:* Now imagine being at work. It's last Wednesday when you had the problem that you told me about with Jeff. You're pointing out his error and asking him to please do it over. He's blowing up and telling you how he doesn't respect your opinion. Now you can focus in on what you are thinking and feeling as you imagine this. (pause) And now you can share with me your thoughts and feelings.

*Alice:* He's right. I don't know what I'm talking about. I feel guilty, like I have no right to use my power over someone else. I know where that comes from. My father and mother always looked down upon people who were aggressive, like they were bad people. I guess that's why I married my husband. He was always so mild mannered. But that made me feel like I was "bad." It was so easy to get my own way with him. He never fought back. But there was no joy in winning. I'd always feel guilty about winning, like I had no right.

*Therapist:* Okay. I see where some of your depression is coming from. It's guilt. We'll come back to this, but now go back to that scene in your office. What's happening now, after Jeff answers back?

*Alice:* Nothing. I'm frozen. I don't say anything. I just go back to my office feeling awful.

*Therapist:* What are you thinking and feeling as you go back to your office?

*Alice:* I can't stand myself! I hate myself! I'm despicable for being so weak! I shouldn't have let him get away with that.

*Therapist:* I can see why you get so depressed. You can't win. If you're assertive you feel guilty, and if you don't act assertive you hate yourself for acting weak. We need to work on resolving this conflict.

Thereafter Alice was able to monitor her depressive thoughts on her own. Her self-monitoring disclosed that she frequently engaged in self-castigation for things like not cleaning her house and lying in bed, and she thought of herself as helpless and hopeless. After pinpointing these specific self-defeating patterns of thinking, the therapist was able to proceed to the next step, cognitive restructuring.

## Cognitive Restructuring

Providing clients with insight about their self-defeating thoughts can have therapeutic value. However, usually such insight does not automatically produce change. Most clients have to be shown how to change their self-defeating thoughts, feelings, and behavior. Although there are many different methods of producing cognitive change (see Golden & Dryden, 1986), the following ones are the most compatible with hypnosis and the easiest for both clients and therapists to learn.

*The Two-Column Method.* Without prior hypnotic induction, the client is instructed to divide a page in half. On one side of the page the client lists his or her negative thoughts or self-suggestions, and, in the other column, the client lists a positive constructive suggestion for each negative thought. The client is instructed to list therapeutic suggestions that will counteract the depressive

Table 3.1. Sample Two – column Method
Situation: Confrontation with Jeff at Work

| Negative Thoughts | Therapeutic Suggestions |
|---|---|
| 1. He's right. I don't know what I'm talking about. | 1. I know my work. I know when some one is goofing off or not doing the job well. Jeff often tries to get through his work with the least amount of time and effort on his part and is often careless. |
| 2. I have no right to use my power over him. | 2. I'm not misusing my power. I'm doing my job. |
| 3. To be aggressive is bad and I'm bad. | 3. I'm not bad nor was I being aggressive. I was being assertive and doing my job. |
| 4. I can't stand myself when I back down. I'm despicable for being so weak. | 4. Sometimes I back down but at other times I'm assertive. My goal is to be more assertive. But sometimes I won't be assertive because I'm scared or in conflict. That's weakness but it doesn't make me despicable. It only means I need to work on this, which I can. |
| 5. It's hopeless, I'll never change. I don't do anything right. | 5. That's absurd. I used to do many things well before I became depressed. I will get better. I can learn to be more assertive. It's not hopeless. There's a way to get over this. |

effect of the negative thoughts. These positive therapeutic suggestions will serve as hypnotic suggestions during hetero- and self- hypnosis. Furthermore, these suggestions can be employed by the client without a prior hypnotic induction whenever he or she needs immediate help, such as when feeling depressed. See Table 3.1 for an example of the two- column method. Alice, the client whose negative thoughts and therapeutic suggestions are presented in Table 3.1, was discussed in the section on evocative imagery. In her case, some of the negative thoughts were elicited through imagery under hypnosis, and others were later identified through self-monitoring. Most clients, at least initially, need the help of their therapists in constructing a list of therapeutic suggestions. Later they can learn to use the two-column method on their own. In Alice's case, the therapeutic suggestions listed in Table 3.1 were formulated through a collaboration between therapist and client. This work took place without any hypnotic induction. The therapist asked questions like "Do you really think Jeff is right, that you don't know what you are talking about?" Alice's immediate response to this question was "Of course not, I know my work." She was encouraged to elaborate further, and her response was written down by the therapist. At other times, when she had difficulty reevaluating her negative thoughts, the therapist offered more assistance. For example, he pointed out "You're not misusing your power, you're doing your job."

*Imaginal Rehearsal.* Through the use of imagery, clients can be helped to anticipate and practice coping with difficult situations. Therapeutic suggestions that guide the client in thinking, feeling, and acting in the problematic situation are given during the imagery.

As an illustration of imaginal rehearsal, Alice will once again be used as an example. As you might recall, Alice put herself in a double bind by feeling guilty when she was assertive and condemning herself when she was unassertive. As outlined, her self-defeating patterns of thinking were identified, and more rational constructive thoughts were developed for use as therapeutic suggestions. During hypnosis, the following suggestions were given:

> Alice, imagine you're at work. You've just gone over Jeff's work and, as you would expect, he's been careless and has made numerous mistakes. You keep in mind that you know what's got to be done and that his work in its present form is unacceptable. Your job is to give him constructive feedback so that the quality of his work will improve. So you make several suggestions gently but firmly. You say something like 'Jeff, I like how you prepared the figures on the Jones account. They're very clear and organized. I think you could do the same with the Smith account.'
> Now imagine his getting defensive and saying 'Get off my case. The way I prepared them was just fine for Mr. Grant, my previous supervisor. Why are you always on my back?'
> You anticipated this response. You keep in mind your goal is to be more assertive and not to back down. It's okay for you to be more assertive. It's your job and you have every right to ask him to make corrections. You hold your ground and simply repeat your request. . . . 'Jeff, I'd like you to make these revisions.' You feel good about having been more assertive.
> But now you know that no one is perfect. Sometimes you'll slip and not be assertive. Imagine another incident with Jeff, where you back down but you don't hate yourself. You remind yourself that you're human and change takes time and that, even when you are unsuccessful in being assertive, it does not mean you are hopeless. In fact, it provides you with an excellent opportunity to work on accepting yourself. You are worthwhile even when you make mistakes or fail to achieve assertive goals. Either way you can't lose. You will either be assertive and feel good about that, or, if you are not assertive on a particular occasion, you will keep in mind that this was only one occasion. There will be others, and you are worthwhile even when you don't do as well as you would like.

In addition to the imaginal rehearsal under hypnosis, the therapist would role-play with Alice to give her further practice in being assertive. Her homework assignments were to listen to tape recordings of her hypnotherapy sessions and the role plays between her and her therapist, to give herself therapeutic suggestions (with or without a prior hypnotic induction) whenever she found herself starting to feel depressed, and to put her assertiveness skills into practice. Within 2 months, without help from

medication, Alice reported feeling better, and she had started to once again
enjoy some of life's pleasures.

## SUMMARY

In this chapter, we have described and illustrated how a variety of
hypnotherapeutic interventions — alert hypnosis, time projection, and
cognitive–behavioral hypnotherapy — can be effectively combined to treat
depression. Each technique can be adapted to the specific preferences of the
client.

# Chapter 4

# Hypnotherapy for Fears, Phobias, and Stress-Related Disorders

Emotional disorders, which are variously labeled anxiety, fear, phobias, and stress reactions, are perhaps the most common of the neuroses. Although anxiety and fear can be useful motivators, they can also cause untold misery and suffering. This chapter will describe the nature of these disorders and several different treatment approaches that can be used to overcome them. The treatment techniques will be illustrated by case examples.

## DISTINCTIVE FEATURES OF ANXIETY, FEAR, PHOBIAS, AND STRESS

It is important to distinguish among anxiety, fear, phobias, and stress. Anxiety and fear in particular are terms often used interchangeably. Some theorists (e.g., Beck & Emery, 1985) have argued that fear is a cognitive process, whereas anxiety is an emotional reaction. Fear, they state, is a cognitive appraisal of a threatening situation that might occur in the future. When the individual is placed in the threatening situation, the fear is activated, and the subsequent emotional reaction is labeled anxiety. Phobias are particularly intense, unrealistic fears characterized by avoidance of the feared object. Stress is the body's viseral response to demands made upon it, and the response tends to be the same regardless of the nature of the stressor. Although these terms all refer to different states with different origins, they have one thing in common: They all involve emotional arousal. This fact has important treatment implications and means that many of the same treatment techniques can be used for all.

# FUNCTIONS OF ANXIETY, FEARS, PHOBIAS, AND STRESS

What are the long-term functions of these emotional states? The original fight–flight reaction suggested that people flee if fighting is not likely to be successful. Beck and Emery (1985) argued that anxiety is a protective mechanism that acts as a warning signal of the individual's vulnerability to physical dangers or social sanctions. Phobias obviously result in avoidance of potentially (to the individual) dangerous situations. Thus, anxiety, fear, and phobias can be seen as avoidance strategies that contribute to the individual's, and therefore the race's, ultimate survival. Similarly, stress reactions can also be seen as warning signals that the body is dangerously overextended, and they probably contribute to long-term survival as well.

Although anxiety, fear, phobias, and stress reactions might serve a legitimate function by discouraging physically or socially dangerous behavior, they might also discourage ordinary risk taking and assertive behavior. The person who sees potential danger in everything is thus prevented from learning or performing new behavior. Within reasonable bounds, anxiety can be a motivator for increased activity. However, whereas a moderate anxiety level can be a stimulus, a high anxiety level can paralyze activity. Similarly, whereas a life of too little stress can result in boredom and ennui, too much stress can result in serious depletion of bodily and emotional resources and even death. Anxiety, fear, phobias, and stress reactions can also be seen as ways of avoiding areas in which one's competency is in doubt. People are typically anxious about situations they feel they will not handle well, and the anxiety generally leads to avoidance of these situation. It is important to note, however, that such people might not actually lack competence but only perceive themselves as lacking it. They could therefore be prevented from learning that they are, in fact, competent.

In summary, anxiety, fear, phobias, and stress reactions can be seen as legitimate, survival-oriented responses to potentially dangerous situations or those for which the individual lacks adequate coping mechanisms. However, reality is not always correctly perceived. People, because of their prior learning experiences, might continuously be responding to a wide variety of situations as though they were dangerous when, in fact, they are not. In addition, although they might in fact, lack coping strategies in certain situations, they also might possess more than they realize. Emotional reactions such as anxiety can be potentially valuable so long as they are not increased too rapidly, are not too prolonged, and are at an optimal level for the individual and so long as the person perceives that he or she can cope with the situation.

# TREATMENT OF ANXIETY, FEARS, AND STRESS DISORDERS: GENERAL CONSIDERATIONS

The treatment of anxiety, fears, and stress disorders can focus on a variety of issues. Treatment can be directed at modification of the environment, to reduce the occurrence of events likely to produce stress and anxiety disorders. It can be directed at reducing the anxiety or fear directly, through techniques such as hypnotic desensitization, so that the client will be more likely to enter troublesome situations and learn that he or she is able to cope more than was initially thought. Treatment can also be directed toward helping a client, through techniques such as cognitive restructuring, to re-interpret the problematic situation as less dangerous than originally thought. Or, the therapist might teach the client new coping strategies, such as self-hypnosis, for the purpose of increasing his or her self-efficacy and to enable him or her to handle anxiety-producing situations better.

Certain adjunctive techniques can also be used. It has often been noted that physical exercise is effective in reducing anxiety and stress, as well as depression. Clients can be encouraged to engage in moderate exercise in line with their physical conditions. In general this should be done in conjunction with a physician's recommendation. Stimulants such as caffeine, nicotine, and drugs and depressants such as alcohol can contribute to anxiety and stress. Ironically, however, these substances are often used in the first place to reduce stress, thus leading to a vicious cycle of substance use and increased anxiety. Use of such substances should be assessed, and programs for intake reduction should be developed in conjunction with the client.

# STRESS-RELATED SYMPTOMS

There are a number of anxiety and stress-related symptoms it is important to recognize. There is often a feeling of tightness in several of the skeletal muscles as well as in the chest and the diaphram. The individual might experience difficulty breathing. There might also be concentration problems and difficulty focusing on task-relevant behavior. Stress and anxiety are also characterized by *hypervigilance*, in which the person pays abnormally close attention to self and the environment. Physiologically, stress and anxiety can result in increased heart rate and blood pressure, decreased skin temperature in the hands and feet, and increased sweating. It is important to note that stress and anxiety can lead to physical symptoms, such as lowered resistance to illness, tiredness, and ulcers. However, the methods to be described later can be used for all these symptoms.

# HYPNOTHERAPY OF ANXIETY, PHOBIAS, AND STRESS DISORDERS

There are three ways in which hypnosis can be used to reduce anxiety reactions and stress. The first is relaxation and systematic desensitization, accompanied by hypnotic suggestions for anxiety reduction. Guided imagery can also be useful. As mentioned earlier, stress reactions, as well as anxiety and phobias, have one thing in common: heightened emotional arousal. This fact is important, for it means that any technique that reduces arousal has the effect of reducing anxiety and stress as well. The second is the use of cognitive restructuring in self-hypnosis as a general coping strategy for anxiety and stress reduction. The third is the use of hypnosis as a technique for uncovering the sources of the anxiety or fear.

## Relaxation

Relaxation is a simple, easy-to-use technique that can help reduce anxiety and stress from a number of sources. Although it is relatively simple, a few pointers are helpful. A more complete discussion of hypnotic relaxation can be found in chapter 2.

Many people make the mistake of thinking that practicing relaxation at one time will protect them from experiencing anxiety and tension at a later time. However, relaxing at 8:00 a.m. does not reduce one's anxiety at 10:00! To benefit from relaxation procedures, it is important to apply them at the time that one is beginning to feel anxious. The most effective method of using relaxation is to nip the anxiety in the bud before it has an opportunity to build up and become overwhelming. Once the anxiety has become overwhelming, it is difficult to relax. Alternatively, clients can be taught to use the earliest signs of anxiety and tension as cues, or signals, to begin using relaxation procedures.

One can develop skill at coping with anxiety by first practicing relaxation under ideal conditions: no distractions and with one's discomfort level low. A subjective rating scale can be used that ranges from 0–100. Let 0 on this scale, called a Subjective Units of Discomfort Scale (SUDS), equal no anxiety, and let 100 represent the worst state of panic possible. Ideally, one should begin practicing relaxation when one's SUDS level is between 20 and 30, a fairly comfortable level. After the client is able to relax from that level, he or she is ready to begin from higher levels.

Some amount of discomfort is natural. A normal level of stress or tension is about 25–35 SUDS. So, be careful to avoid setting unrealistic goals with clients, such as trying to attain a state of total tranquillity (0 SUDS) through the day.

## Hypnotic Desensitization

Desensitization is a technique in which one confronts one's anxiety or fears in a gradual one-step-at-a-time manner. The person's anxieties or fears are rank ordered from easiest, or least anxiety producing, to most difficult, or most anxiety producing. Usually this rank ordering is done in conjunction with the client. Although standardized hierarchies have been used, it is best to work with clients in developing individual hierarchies. Hypnotic desensitization differs from traditional systematic desensitization in that hypnotic induction procedures, as described in chapter 2, are used to initially relax the client. The therapist then asks the client to imagine the first scene on the hierarchy while remaining in a hypnotic relaxed state. If the client is able to do this and remain relaxed, the therapist asks the client to imagine the next scene. This continues unless the client becomes anxious, at which point the therapist instructs the client to employ relaxation procedures, hypnotic suggestions, or both to reduce the anxiety. If the client is unsuccessful in reducing the anxiety aroused by a particular item on the hierarchy, the therapist returns to the last successfully mastered step. With continued practice, the client is enabled to move up on the anxiety hierarchy while remaining in a relaxed hypnotic state. The therapist might ask the client to imagine himself or herself either coping with the situation or mastering it. Coping imagery differs from mastery imagery in that one anticipates feeling some anxiety but then imagines oneself coping with it. With mastery imagery, one imagines oneself succeeding without any anxiety; for example, an actor imagining that he or she is giving a great performance without feeling anxious. After mastering or coping with an item on the hierarchy, the client is instructed to confront the situation in reality. This is called *in vivo* desensitization. The following list is an example of an anxiety hierarchy for someone with job interview anxiety:

1. Buying newspaper — 25 SUDS (least anxiety producing)
2. Checking help-wanted ads — 30 SUDS
3. Preparing resume — 35 SUDS
4. Mailing resume — 40 SUDS
5. Visiting employment office — 45 SUDS
6. Telephoning and answering uninteresting ads — 50 SUDS
7. Telephoning and answering interesting ads — 55 SUDS
8. Filling out job applications — 60 SUDS
9. Asking for references — 65 SUDS
10. Thinking about going for a job interview — 70 SUDS
11. Taking an employment test — 75 SUDS
12. The night before an interview — 80 SUDS
13. The morning of an interview — 85 SUDS
14. Waiting to be interviewed — 90 SUDS

15. Being interviewed — 95 SUDS

The use of hypnotic desensitization can be illustrated by the case of Fred. Fred came to see the therapist (F.F.) reporting an intense fear of flying. This was especially debilitating because he was required to take two or three business trips a year that necessitated air travel. Because he anticipated severe anxiety, panic, and embarrassment about flying, he would either try to postpone or cancel these trips or travel by train, a very time-consuming alternative. When he did fly, he experienced high levels of anxiety based on thoughts that he would "lose control," that others would notice his distress, and that he would experience extreme embarrassment. In addition, he feared the plane would crash.

A systematic desensitization treatment was developed for Fred. The therapist and client together constructed a hierarchy of anxiety-producing events concerned with flying. The events were rated from 0–100, 0 indicating no anxiety about the situation and 100 representing the highest level of anxiety. The hierarchy consisted of these items:

|    | Situation                                  | SUDS |
|----|--------------------------------------------|------|
| 1  | Driving to the airport                     | 35   |
| 2  | Boarding the airplane                      | 40   |
| 3  | Lights and sounds in the passenger cabin   | 45   |
| 4  | Finding seat and fastening seatbelt        | 50   |
| 5  | Airplane hatch closing                     | 55   |
| 6  | Landing                                    | 60   |
| 7  | Plane taxiing on the runway                | 65   |
| 8  | Take-off                                   | 70   |
| 9  | Sharp turn while aloft                     | 75   |
| 10 | Turbulence in flight                       | 80   |
| 11 | Feeling anxious while airborne             | 90   |

The hypnotic desensitization process taught the client to reduce his anxiety level in the feared situation through self-relaxation and coping suggestions. The following are examples of some of the desensitization scenes (corresponding to the situations in the list just given) presented to Fred during hypnosis.

Scene 5. Imagine that you have already boarded the airplane, found your seat, and fastened your seat belt. Now you hear the hatch door being shut. Now, as you imagine this, where would you rate your anxiety on the 0–100 scale? (Client reports no anxiety.)

Scene 8. Now imagine that the plane is set for take-off. You hear the high pitch of the engines as they rev up for take-off. Then the plane begins to accelerate, going faster and faster, hitting the bumps along the runway. Finally the plane lifts off the ground. You feel the sharp ascent and pressure against your body. In this scene, rate your anxiety level. (Client reports, 40, a moderate level of anxiety.) All right. See if you are aware of any anxiety-producing thoughts such as "I am trapped" or "the plane is going to crash!" You don't give them any special significance. They are to be expected. You distract yourself from them by reading and listening to music and you use your relaxation techniques to calm yourself. . . . relaxing now. Not taking these thoughts seriously. Still in the plane, but calmer now. Relaxing away the anxiety. All right. Rate your anxiety again. (Client reports 0.) Good.

Scene 11. Now imagine you are at cruising altitude. You start to feel anxious. Rate your anxiety level. (Client reports 60.)

All right. You remind yourself that, even if you are anxious, you'll be all right. You'll get through it. Eventually it will pass. Even if you can't relax it all away and are still anxious, you can cope with it. You can use your relaxation techniques to keep the anxiety down to a manageable level. Also keep in mind that other people probably can't tell that you're anxious, but, even if they could, they wouldn't necessarily disapprove of you. But even if they did, you don't need their approval. Now, once again, rate your anxiety level. (Client reports 20.)

Very good! You have succeeded in controlling and reducing your anxiety. Your confidence about flying will be greater now. You can apply your self-hypnotic techniques the next time you fly. Hypnosis, relaxation, and coping self-suggestions will give you confidence and control. Yes, confidence and control.

Fred's home practice of self-hypnotic desensitization further prepared him for flying. In the 6-month period following hypnotic desensitization treatment, the client made three flights and reported effective control and reduction of anxiety.

## COGNITIVE—BEHAVIORAL HYPNOTHERAPY

Hypnosis can be used for the relief of symptoms or as part of a more comprehensive approach that also includes insight into the underlying causes of a symptom. Insight alone will not cure a symptom, but it can help in understanding what is maintaining a symptom and thereby aid in its removal. However, problems are not invariably rooted deep in childhood. They can come from self-defeating and negative thoughts that are suggested to oneself repeatedly. Araoz (1981) has pointed out that this process is a form of negative self-hypnosis. Cognitive–behavioral hypnotherapy is particularly useful for overcoming negative self-hypnosis because the positive internal dialogue it fosters is in direct opposition to the negative self-talk characteristic of negative self-hypnosis. As discussed in chapter 3, cognitive–behavioral hypnotherapy can be subdivided into two basic steps: the uncovering or identification of self-defeating thoughts (negative self-hypnosis) and cognitive restructuring.

## Uncovering Techniques

Before modifying maladaptive thoughts, it is important that the therapist help clients recognize them. Pinpointing one's anxiety creating thoughts and fantasies is not that difficult. With very little training and practice, most people can "tune" into their "internal dialogues" and observe their thoughts and fantasies. These are not usually buried away deep in the "unconscious," as many people believe. A better word to describe them might be "subconscious" (just below the surface of awareness). Although we do not usually pay much attention to our thoughts, fantasies, and daydreams, we can become aware of them simply by focusing attention on them. One does not need to be in a trance or even need to use relaxation techniques to discover them. Nevertheless, some people find that relaxation procedures help them confront anxiety-producing thoughts and fantasies that they are usually afraid to face.

One technique that can be used with or without prior hypnotic induction is to ask clients to recall a problematic situation and to recollect what they were thinking and imagining just before experiencing anxiety. Alternatively, teach clients to use self-monitoring, in which they are instructed to keep a log and to record the situations, thoughts, and fantasies that trigger anxiety. They are advised to make entries in their logs whenever they feel anxious and to observe the thoughts present in their minds at that time or recall what they were thinking just prior to experiencing anxiety.

Evocative imagery can also be used to discover anxiety-producing thoughts. Clients can be instructed, either during hypnosis or without the benefit of a prior hypnotic induction procedure, to imagine themselves doing what they are afraid of doing (for example initiating a conversation with a stranger in a social situation). Ask them to wait until they feel some discomfort, then report whatever thoughts and fantasies come to their minds (such as seeing themselves being rejected). Later the therapist and the clients can use the material thus generated to construct self-hypnotic suggestions. See chapter 3 for an illustration of the use of evocative imagery.

If imagery and self-monitoring techniques fail to disclose anxiety-producing thoughts and fantasies, exposure to the real situation can be used for this purpose. The idea is to elicit anxiety and to observe what thoughts and fantasies trigger it.

## Cognitive Restructuring

The next step is rewriting the anxiety-creating script, replacing self-defeating and negative suggestions (that is one's negative self-hypnosis) with constructive and positive suggestions. A good method of developing these therapeutic suggestions is through reevaluation of one's thoughts. This method derives from Rational–Emotive Therapy (RET) and other forms of cognitive behavioral therapy and is called *cognitive restructuring*. A simple cognitive-restructuring procedure for creating these suggestions is the two-column method (see Table 4.1). As noted earlier it consists of dividing a page in half, then listing the anxiety-producing thoughts in the first column and constructing therapeutic suggestions for each anxiety-producing thought in the second column. The goal is to help the client construct a list of suggestions that will serve as hypnotic suggestions during hetero- and self-hypnosis.

An example of the use of the two-column method for constructing hypnotic suggestions is the case of Jim, who came to therapy for relief of anxiety attacks. He reported that they occurred while he was driving his car.

To provide direct symptom relief, the therapist (W.G.) taught Jim relaxation techniques for reducing anxiety. As part of a comprehensive approach, Jim was instructed to observe and keep a written record of his thoughts and the fantasies that preceded and aroused the anxiety. It soon became clear that Jim became anxious while driving to school because he daydreamed and worried about his future. He had ambivalent feelings about his future, because he did not really want to continue in business administration but wanted to train as a musician. The obstacle was his anxiety about failure. Although he was already a talented musician, he worried about failing, thereby creating anxiety and tension. By avoiding the risk of pursuing what he really wanted, he found himself caught in a conflict: worrying about failing as a musician and worrying about being unhappy because he was not pursuing a career as a musician. Hence, Jim's therapy not only focused on symptom relief through hypnotic relaxation but also dealt with his anxiety about failure.

Through self-monitoring, Jim discovered the following anxiety-producing thoughts: He would definitely fail as a musician; if he failed at music he would "be a failure" and would then have no other options or happiness in life. Using the two-column method, Jim and his therapist constructed

Table 4. Sample Two-column Method

| Negative Thoughts | Therapeutic Suggestions |
|---|---|
| 1. I will fail as a musician (a self-fulfilling prophecy). | 1. I have a good chance of succeeding at some level in music because I already am a good musician. |
| 2. If I fail at music, I will be a failure. | 2. Even if I fail as a professional musician, I'm not a failure. I already have succeeded to some degree, not only at music, but other things as well. |
| 3. If I don't make it as a professional musician, then I'll have no other options or happiness in life. | 3. If I can't succeed financially as a musician, I can pursue some other career, and I can still keep music as a hobby and do other things for pleasure. |

therapeutic suggestions that could be used during hypnosis. During therapy sessions, Jim's therapist repeated the positive suggestions, as outlined in Table 4.1.

Jim was then instructed to use these suggestions for self-hypnosis and was successful in using hypnotic relaxation to reduce his anxiety. He changed schools and returned to music school.

## Insight-oriented Hypnotherapy

A large part of psychodynamic approaches to psychotherapy is the uncovering or, recovery of repressed or forgotten past events and feelings. According to psychodynamic theory, this material is highly emotionally charged, which is why it was originally repressed. Often it consists of reactions and feelings that were appropriate at a much earlier stage of development but are not appropriate for adults. Yet this old material can continue to dominate an individual's reactions to adult situations. In certain cases, recovery of these past emotional reactions and their examination in the light of an adult perspective can significantly reduce the power these events have over current functioning. Thus, psychodynamic psychotherapists spend significant time discussing past events and feelings in their clients' lives and interpreting them in the light of present reality.

Hypnosis can be of great help in the uncovering of repressed or forgotten emotional material that the client believes is exercising an effect on his or her current life. Because one effect of the hypnotic trance state is to bypass resistance, the client's ordinary resistance to the recovery of this material can be significantly reduced. In addition, the heightened concentration that is often evident in hypnosis can aid in focusing on repressed events so that they can be remembered. Hypnotic age regression or age revivification can be an especially powerful tool in uncovering repressed memories.

Age regression and age revivification are similar phenomena, but differ in the degree of simulation in the experience. During an age regression, the subject recalls significant earlier events, but reports them as having happened in the past and generally speaks in the past tense. During this time, the subject acts and feels as an adult. In age revivification, however, the subject acts as a child, talks as a child, talks in the present tense, and otherwise responds exactly as he or she would have at that age. There is thus a degree of realism and immediacy that is not present in age regression. Excellent hypnotic subjects are more likely to achieve age revivification than are poorer hypnotic subjects and to experience the repressed emotional material more powerfully.

There are several ways to use age regression or age revivification in treating anxiety disorders. *First*, it is important to move backward in time in a way that is helpful for the client. Some therapists have counted backward by years, others by the client's age, and still others by asking the client to imagine the leaves of a calendar flipping backward, It is important to choose a method in collaboration with the client, for maximum involvement and motivation. It is often helpful to instruct the client that he or she will always be able to hear the therapist's voice and respond to the therapist's directions, as a sort of life-line. This also provides a rationale for the therapist's presence at an earlier stage in the client's life.

*Second*, the therapist can instruct the client to either talk about emotional material at various ages or use ideomotor signaling. Again, the method used should be chosen in conjunction with the client. Some people seem to feel that if one can talk, one is not really in a trance; for these people, ideomotor signaling should be used. Client talk, if appropriate, is more flexible. The therapist can either instruct the client to relate any significant events at different ages or years or pause at each time period and ask the client for any significant memories. In ideomotor signaling, the therapist can ask the client questions and instruct him or her to, for example, "raise your right index finger if the answer is yes and your left index finger if the answer is no." Obviously, ideomotor signaling is much slower, but it does add to the mystery and ritual of hypnosis, which can enhance motivation and involvement for some subjects. Milton Erickson often instructed subjects to let their unconscious minds guide the choice of which finger would rise, thus making it seem like an involuntary process and perhaps further increasing motivation.

Especially in the case of good hypnotic subjects, recovery of repressed material can lead to a large emotional abreaction. It is thus very important that the hypnotist be a well-qualified therapist who is able to handle emotional reactions easily and quickly. This underscores the previous statement that hypnosis is not a therapy in itself but an adjunctive technique to psychotherapy. A hypnotherapist should be a therapist first and a hypnotist second. Significant material elicited by hypnosis usually should be discussed and integrated in subsequent sessions.

The use of age regression in hypnotherapy can be illustrated by the case of Jane, who sought help from one of the authors (E.T.D.) for an intense fear of the dark. Jane had previously been in therapy for a number of other issues, which she had satisfactorily resolved, and she was now determined to conquer this fear. She reported intense anxiety when alone in the house at night and that she repeatedly checked windows and doors to make sure they were locked. When she could not see everything around her, she reported being afraid something would "get her." She also experienced anxiety when driving home at night. In addition, she would repeatedly wake up screaming at night and require her roomate to sleep on the side of the bed closest to the door. She described herself as a perfectionist, with a strong need to be in control of herself and the situation.

Jane's family background was relatively impoverished. Her father and mother were both dead, her father having died when she was 4 years old. Her mother had been quite ill for many years. She has a sister 18 years older than she and a brother 10 years older. Her relationship with her sister was cordial and that with her brother distant. She reported never really having had a childhood and living in constant fear that her mother would become sick.

An initial hypnotic induction showed Jane to be a good hypnotic subject, satisfactorily completing an arm levitation, although she was worried that had not "done it correctly" (likely due to her perfectionistic tendencies). Because one of her presenting complaints was that she awoke screaming each night, the therapist decided to attack that problem directly. Using an eye-fixation (and subsquent eye-closure) induction technique and descending stairs as a deepening technique, Jane was able to readily enter a trance. A paradoxical hypnotic routine was used in which it was suggested that only those people who were really in control (a desirable attribute for her) could feel secure enough to relinquish control temporarily. Therefore, if she could give up some control, it would indicate that she was more in control. The therapist then suggested that she would be able to gradually lose her fear of the dark, and her frequency of waking up screaming would diminish. Posthypnotic amnesia was suggested. Upon coming out of the trance, Jane was in fact unable to remember what had been said, thus validating that she was a good hypnotic subject.

Assessments in subsequent sessions revealed that her incidents of waking up screaming at night, as monitored by both herself and her roommate, were diminishing. However, she was still afraid of the dark. Therefore, age regression was used to attempt to locate the origin of the fear. Her previous success with hypnosis indicated that she was capable of entering a deep enough trance to use this technique. Jane preferred to be regressed by means of a backward count by her age, rather than by calendar year. She was instructed to report, while in the trance, significant events that she thought might be important to her fear of the dark. At age 8, she reported feeling very dizzy. At age 3, she remembered that she was very much afraid of a dark cellar. Probing indicated that a cousin would take her to her aunt's cellar and turn off the light to terrify her. Jane would then run up the stairs screaming. She described these events in the past tense, which indicated that she experienced an age regression rather than an age revivification. After termination of the trance, she stated that both the dizziness and the remembrance of the dark cellar were new to her.

At the next session, age regression was again employed. Jane was asked to describe her feelings when her cousin turned out the light. She described it as a panicky and helpless feeling of being out of control. While she was in the trance, the therapist talked to her about how children feel helpless because bigger people are so much more powerful. As children grow older, however, they become more powerful but often do not realize that fact. The therapist then said, "and we need not fear as adults the things we feared as children." Upon terminating the trance, the therapist discussed with Jane how her current fear and behavior were similar to what she had experienced at 3 years old. Specifically, she ran screaming up the stairs then, and now she wakes up screaming; she felt helpless then because she could not control the situation, and she feels helpless now when she is not in control. She said that she had not realized before how childhood fears can carry over into adulthood.

Subsequent sessions revealed that she woke up at night very rarely and then did not scream. She reported that she was not afraid of the dark nearly so much. When the fear occurred, she was able to tell herself that the fear was old and groundless, and she then felt better.

This case illustrates several things. *First*, it shows how direct suggestion for symptom remission can sometimes be effective with circumscribed symptoms. *Second*, it shows how age regression can be used to uncover significant repressed or forgotten incidents. *Third*, it shows how these incidents can then be reinterpreted in an adult context to lead to symptom relief. Of course, reinterpreting childhood incidents in an adult framework is common to many therapies. Hypnosis is a way of facilitating this process for some clients. Thus, this case also forcefully illustrates the oft-stated maxim we noted before, that hypnosis is not a therapy in itself but an adjunctive technique to psychotherapy.

## SUMMARY

Hypnosis can be of great help in treating anxiety, fears, and stress-related disorders. In this chapter, we have described several different hypnotherapeutic approaches: simple hypnotic relaxation, hypnotic desensitization, cognitive restructuring, and age regression.

# Chapter 5
# Hypnotherapeutic Pain Control

Contrary to popular opinion, pain is a complex phenomenon. It is not simply a physical sensation but often involves cognitive, perceptual, emotional, behavioral, and interpersonal factors. This chapter will describe some of the more commonly encountered types of pain and discuss hypnotherapeutic methods for controlling pain. First, however, the various factors in pain will be described.

## PHYSICAL FACTORS IN PAIN

We suggest two ways of looking at physical pain. The specificity approach proposes that pain sensations result from the stimulation of specific pain receptors, which are generally considered to be free nerve endings located in body tissues. Although there is a certain surface plausibility to this idea, because we do indeed feel pain at the location of an injury in proportion to the extent of that injury, there are two major problems with this idea. *First*, it fails to explain how people with identical pain syndromes often respond quite differently. *Second*, it cannot account for such phenomena as phantom limb pain, where pain is felt in a missing limb. The gate control theory of pain, developed by Melzack and Wall (1965), proposes that pain impulses from sensory receptors are transmitted to the spinal cord over both large and small fibres. Neural mechanisms in the spinal cord act like a gate that can increase or decrease the flow of nerve impulses. The entire gate control mechanism can be controlled by the central nervous system, thus influencing the experience of pain. It has been shown that intense pain can be relieved by bombarding the central nervous system with nonpainful stimuli, presumably closing the "gate" to painful impulses. However, in chronic pain situations, it is unlikely that the gate can be kept closed indefinitely by such means.

58

# COGNITIVE FACTORS IN PAIN

The way that people think about their pain also influences how it is felt. It is possible to learn to pay less attention to pain by engaging in imagery that is incompatible with the experience of pain, such as by imagining a beach scene. It is also possible to divert attention from painful sensations by focusing attention on one's physical surroundings. One can also focus attention on the part of the body that is experiencing the pain, but in a detached manner. In addition, one can focus on the painful area, but relabel, and therefore redefine, the pain as something else such as pressure. The point is that, by thinking about pain in a different way, either by diversion or by detachment, the experience of pain is thereby changed.

Many people, upon first feeling pain, catastrophize about it. Catastrophizing involves negative thoughts about one's ability to cope with the pain. People who catastrophize about their pain assume that they will not be able to deal with it, or that it will always be present, or that it will get worse. Such thoughts then cause the pain to be felt more intensely, which leads to greater feelings of helplessness, which results in more felt pain, and so on. Interventions that reduce catastrophizing can be helpful in reducing pain.

# PERCEPTUAL FACTORS IN PAIN

It has been noted that people who pay attention to their pain and who are vigilant in their attention to painful sensations are in fact, more aware of their pain. On the other hand, those individuals whose attention is diverted from painful sensations often report feeling no pain at the time. An example is the injured football player who reports pain only after he has ceased playing and has had time to notice that he is hurt. This can be a problem, especially for people who have little to do and therefore have much time and energy to devote to paying attention to their painful sensations. One obvious solution is to give them more to occupy their time and thus help them to pay less attention to their pain.

# EMOTIONAL FACTORS IN PAIN

The experience of pain can cause a great deal of emotionality as well. The most obvious of these emotions in anxiety. People become extremely anxious when they are in pain, especially when the occurrence of the pain cannot be predicted. Under these circumstances, they become anxious as they await the onset of pain, which only intensifies the pain. A pattern is quickly built up in which intermittent pain leads to anxious expectation, which leads to greater perception of pain and more subsequent anxiety. In addition, people often tense their muscles prior to or during pain as a sort of coping strategy. But instead of reducing pain, muscle tension creates additional pain. This is an example of a coping strategy actually making the problem worse. However, individuals generally do not know about other pain-controlling techniques, so they are condemned to do "more of the same." Techniques that reduce anxiety and tension, such as relaxation procedures, can be helpful.

## BEHAVIORAL FACTORS IN PAIN

People also exhibit a number of "pain behaviors" when in pain. These include complaining verbally, avoiding activities, moaning, walking stiffly, holding the painful area, and the like. These activities are initially expressions of pain, but they gradually become cues for pain. That is, eventually the performance of these behaviors serves as a reminder that one is, or should be, in pain. In addition, these behaviors also increase the perception of the pain itself. Again, there is a vicious cycle, in which the pain results in certain behavior, which in turn exacerbates the pain. It becomes important, therefore, in the treatment of pain, that these activities be discontinued.

## INTERPERSONAL FACTORS IN PAIN

The experiences of pain can be socially reinforcing to the individual as well. This is called secondary gain. Pain can be seen as a learned behavior that can be modified by changing the reinforcing consequences. Wilbert Fordyce (1974), in particular, has argued that pain is a learned, reinforced behavior. He suggested that, if behaviors that signal pain are reinforced in the environment, these pain behaviors become more frequent. If they then result in increasing attention from others or avoidance of responsibilities, the individual might be motivated to continue them. Thus, pain behavior originally caused by organic factors can eventually occur, after the organic cause has disappeared, in response to reinforcers from the environment. The therapist should therefore examine the clients environment for possible reinforcers of the experience of pain.

Gallager and Wrobel (1982) have thought of chronic illness behavior (including pain) in terms of the sick-role concept. The sick person, because he or she is not functioning well, is excused from many of the obligations expected of others. They call this *socially legitimized dependency*. Being excused from common social responsibility and receiving increased attention from others can powerfully reinforce pain behaviors, perception of pain, and dependency.

## TYPES OF PAIN

Although many people think of pain as a uniform sensation, differing only in intensity, there are actually several types of pain. For example, Turk, Meichenbaum and Genest (1983) categorized clinical pain into five different types (four of which are listed below). The treatment interventions differ significantly for each type.

1. *Acute pain*. Usually this is time-limited and of less than 6 months duration. It includes postsurgical pain, dental pain, and pain accompanying childbirth. Because acute pain gradually declines in intensity, relaxation techniques and other anxiety reduction procedures are generally sufficient for relief. Psychological factors and secondary gain are usually not present.

2. *Chronic, periodic pain*. This recurs and is intense and intermittent. Examples include migraine headaches and trigeminal neuralgia. Although psychological factors can be present, there is the stronger likelihood of physiological causes. Treatment can focus on symptom relief techniques such as direct suggestions for the reduction of pain or relaxation techniques. Interventions that deal with the more recurrent aspects of the pain can also be helpful, such as hypnotic skills training as described in chapter 2. The fact that the pain is time limited is helpful in that temporary measures do provide relief, although of course they must be repeated when the pain returns. The client must first be disabused of the notion that hypnosis will somehow produce a magic cure, and second, be provided with coping strategies he or she can use in handling the pain when it returns.

3. *Chronic, intractable, benign pain*. Present most of the time, it varies in level of intensity. The primary example is lower-back pain. Here, secondary gain and psychological factors play a large part, often larger than physical factors. Any treatment program must therefore take into account environmental reinforcing variables for continued pain, such as financial compensation and family members. Although the original source of the pain was once physical, interpersonal aspects could now account for most or all of the pain. There are often significant psychological and social benefits to be obtained from remaining in pain. Treatment that is focused only on reducing the pain often fails, because the individual might lose disability benefits or the psychological benefits of the sick role if the pain were to be reduced or eliminated. See chapter 8 on resistance for ways of handling this problem.

4. *Chronic, progressive pain*. Often associated with cancer and other malignancies, this is perhaps the most difficult type of pain to treat successfully. Temporary pain-reducing measures that, according to Melzack and Wall's gate control theory, effectively close the gate might not be effective in keeping it closed. The progressive and constant nature of the pain exhausts the individual's physical and emotional resources and makes it more difficult to keep up the efforts required for pain relief. Anxiety is often a

prominent feature of this type of pain, and simple relaxation is sometimes effective in reducing the anxiety, and therefore the perception of pain. Secondary gain and psychological factors are rarely present, so that treatment can focus directly and effectively on pain relief.

## ASSESSMENT OF PAIN

Although pencil-and-paper tests for assessing pain are available, we find it more useful to assess pain through self-monitoring procedures. Clients are instructed to monitor the specific situations in which they experience pain, what they are thinking and feeling when they experience pain, and how they react to the pain and to record the intensity and duration of the pain and the amount of medication they use. See Table 5.1 for a sample pain log for self-monitoring purposes. Through self-monitoring it is possible to identify factors that produce or increase pain such as anxiety and tension that results in headaches, as well as those that maintain or reinforce it such as passivity, avoidance of responsibilities, and drug dependency.

Another valuable advantage of self-monitoring is that it allows the clinician to measure pain in terms of its frequency, intensity, and duration, thus making it possible to monitor the client's progress. Individuals in pain understandably seek immediate relief and expect hypnosis to magically eliminate the pain. However, for the majority of patients, hypnosis reduces, but does not totally eliminate, pain. Progress in hypnotherapy often occurs in small steps, as opposed to dramatically occurring after one or two sessions. Clients need to learn how to induce and apply self-hypnosis so they can manage pain as needed. When data is available as a result of continuous ongoing self-monitoring, the client can be shown that progress is in fact being made. Often change is very subtle, perhaps observed in only one area as a reduction in the frequency, the intensity, or the duration of pain, or it might only consist of a reduction in the amount of medication needed to control the pain. Clients with chronic pain can easily become discouraged and slip into hopelessness, particularly at the beginning of treatment or when they experience setbacks.

Data demonstrating a tendency to progress can be presented to clients to prevent them from becoming discouraged. The advantage of having several measures (for example frequency, duration, and intensity of pain and amount of medication used) is that you increase the likelihood of identifying progress, if there is any to observe. Progress might be reflected on only one of the measures at the beginning of treatment. For example, the first change that might take place in a client's headaches is that they decrease in intensity even though they occur just as frequently and last as long as they did prior to treatment. Or, headaches might occur with the same frequency and intensity but be shorter in duration as a result of the client's using self-hypnosis.

Table 5.1. Sample Pain Log for Self-Monitoring of Pain

| DATE | TIME | SITUATION | THOUGHTS | FEELINGS | ACTIONS | INTENSITY (1–10) | DURATION | MEDICATION |
|---|---|---|---|---|---|---|---|---|
| 5/1 | 7:30a.m. | Lying in bed thinking about doing the day's chores | It's going to be a bad day. I know I'll be in pain if I try to be active. | Anxiety | Stayed in bed for several hours | 8 | 5 hours | 5 mg valium 1 tylenol (with codeine) |
| 5/1 | 2:00a.m. | Thinking about how Harold (her husband) will criticize me for not accomplishing anything | He's going to be mad and we'll have an ugly scene. I can't stand the way he treats me. It's hopeless. Nothing will ever change. | Anxiety Anger Depression | Tried to get some work done | 10 | 2 hours | 5 mg valium 2 tylenol |
| 5/1 | 8:00a.m. | Fight with Harold | He just doesn't understand me, and he never will. | Anger Depression | Went to bed early — 9:00p.m. | 9 | 1 hour | Dalmane 2 tylenol |

Another possibility is that initial change is observed as a decrease in medication because the client is using self-hypnosis instead. The main point is that, unless you are measuring these changes, both you and the client could be unaware of therapeutic progress and give up prematurely.

## TREATMENT OF PAIN: GENERAL CONSIDERATIONS

Before attempting to remove pain by hypnosis, it is extremely important that the client be medically evaluated to insure that the pain is not due to a condition requiring medical treatment. Pain is the body's warning system that something is wrong; to remove the signaling system without removing the source of the pain by medical treatment is certainly unethical and possibly dangerous. Only if medical diagnosis has shown that the pain is not of organic origin or, if it is not treatable medically is hypnotic treatment indicated. Thus, pain control should normally be done in conjunction with or by referral from a physician. For the same reason, it is generally not desirable to remove all pain sensations from an injury. Pain usually serves a valid purpose, either organically or psychologically, and it is wise to leave some residual feeling.

Anxiety and tension are often associated problems in pain control, especially for chronic pain, particularly of the progressive nature. As the pain becomes more and more uncontrollable and unpredictable, the individual's coping resources diminish, and anxiety and tension increase as he or she braces for the next pain attack. Unfortunately, however, this increased tension and anxiety lead to a heightened perception of pain, thus beginning a maladaptive spiral. Therefore, anxiety- and tension-reducing techniques (see chapter 4) such as relaxation procedures often have the effect of reducing pain sensations as well.

There is considerable controversy regarding the effect of hypnotic capacity (that is, the ability to respond to suggestions) on successful pain control through hypnotic methods. There is also disagreement as to whether hypnotic ability is a stable individual difference variable at all. This issue was discussed in chapters 1 and 2. A consideration of the argument goes well beyond the scope of this book, however. Situational factors such as the client–hypnotherapist relationship, client motivation, and expectation of change all influence hypnotizability. Gargiulo (1983) found that subjects receiving hypnotic skills training demonstrated increased pain tolerance, decreased pain ratings, and greater use of positive coping strategies than subjects not receiving hypnotic skills training. Hypnotic skills training had a greater effect on pain reduction and tolerance than either hypnotic susceptibility or hypnotic induction. He also found that hypnotic skills training could modify hypnotic susceptibility to some extent, although susceptibility pre scores were the best predictors of susceptibility post scores.

The evidence seems to indicate that people possess hypnotic ability to a greater or lesser extent and skills training can modify this. Certain techniques, such as dissociation, transformation, and anesthesia require high hypnotizability, whereas others such as distraction, relaxation, and analgesia do not. Although it is true that good hypnotic subjects can enter a deeper trance more readily and therefore control a more intense pain sooner, it is also true that most therapeutic work can be done in a light or medium trance. Hypnosis can be useful for relatively poor subjects if motivation and confidence in the treatment are sufficiently high. Poor subjects can also be taught to be adequate subjects (although not hypnotic virtuosos) if they receive skills training.

It is particularly important in treating pain via hypnotic procedures to inform clients thay they cannot realistically, in most cases, expect to have their pain disappear immediately, completely, and forever. As discussed earlier, hypnosis has been invested to some extent with magical qualities by large segments of the lay public, and they often expect that massive gains will result quickly with minimal effort on their part. It is important to correct these misconceptions, so that clients will not be disappointed in the future.

## TREATMENT OF PAIN: SPECIFIC TECHNIQUES

Several specific hypnotic pain control techniques have been developed and used. Some have general utility, whereas others are particularly useful with certain kinds of pain problems. Some of the more common techniques will now be described, along with suggestions as to their best applicability. Examples of hypnotic routines that can be used while the client is in trance will be given, although readers are urged to modify these or develop their own as situational needs dictate. No standard routine is applicable to all individuals.

## Hypnotic Relaxation

Relaxation procedures as described in chapter 2 are often very effective in controlling pain, especially acute pain. This is so because relaxation reduces the anxiety and tension that often make painful sensations worse. If anxiety and tension can be diminished, the perception of pain can also be reduced. In addition, the individual learns a coping strategy that can be used whenever the pain returns and acquires hope that the pain can be controlled in the future. Especially in cases where the pain is due to a temporary situation like surgery, this might be all that is necessary. Because almost everyone, whether a good hypnotic subject or not, can benefit from relaxation, this procedure has much to recommend it. To avoid client disappointment if he or she has come expecting to be hypnotized, the relaxation procedure can be referred to as hypnosis, as discussed in chapter 2.

## Direct Suggestion

For highly motivated clients with low to moderate pain intensity who have moderate to high hypnotizability, direct suggestion for pain removal or reduction could be effective. However, this technique has limited applicability for several reasons. *First,* it is less likely to be successful if the pain intensity is great. *Second,* it does not give the client coping strategies, and, for that reason its effectiveness is likely to diminish over time. *Third,* it requires a highly motivated subject with fairly good trance capacity. *Fourth,* it sets the hypnotherapist up to fail, with consequent reduction in credibility. Of course, direct suggestion for pain control should only be used when a medical examination has ruled out remedial organic treatment. It is usually preferable to suggest that the pain will be reduced rather than removed. This procedure is best used with acute pain that has an organic basis. Clients with psychogenic pain might defeat hypnotic suggestions. Chronic pain, especially of the progressive variety, might simply be too overwhelming for this technique to work. To use this procedure, first put the client into a trance and then direct him or her as follows:

> And as you find yourself feeling more comfortable and more relaxed, you will discover that your painful sensations are becoming less and less noticeable. You will find your pain gradually diminishing until you can barely (or cannot) feel it. And as you relax more and more (or sink deeper and deeper into a trance), you will become more and more comfortable in all ways. As you become more and more comfortable, you will begin to feel happy and peaceful. And you will discover when you come out of your trance that, much to your surprise, your pain has (almost) disappeared.

## Indirect Suggestion

Indirect suggestion for pain removal or reduction is similar to direct suggestion, except that it is worded in a fashion that does not challenge the client to resist. Words like *comfortable, relaxed, letting go,* and *peaceful* are stressed, and the individual is encouraged (not instructed) to allow (not cause) the pain to gradually disappear. Often embedded suggestions are used, especially by Ericksonian hypnotherapists (see chapter 8). Indirect suggestion might be more effective with psychogenic pain than direct suggestion, because the subtlety of the procedure tends to reduce client resistance. A particularly good example of an indirect hypnotic routine for pain reduction can be found in Healy and Dowd (1986).

## Transformation of Pain

Pain can also be transformed by hypnosis. Two kinds of transformations have been used: those in which the pain is actually moved to another part of the body and those in which the pain itself is transformed into another type of sensation that is easier to live with. The first involves a physical transformation, whereas the second involves a psychological shift in the meaning of the pain. Each will be discussed in turn.

In physical transformation of pain, the pain is moved to a part of the body that is less central to the individual's activities or to a location that is so ridiculous that the person is enabled to treat it in a humorous fashion, thus making it easier to view the pain in a more detached manner. For example, lower-back pain could be transferred to the big toe, where it interferes less with daily activities. Or a headache could be moved to the little finger of the right hand or, more humorously, the left earlobe. This procedure is especially valuable is cases of chronic, intractable, benign pain, where there is often a need to retain the pain for psychological reasons. The client is thus not asked to give up the pain, but only to transform it. Often it is helpful to ask clients where they would like to move their pain to, in order to involve them in the process.

Physical transformation of pain is accomplished as follows. After the subject is placed in a trance, he or she is instructed to touch the painful part of the body with (usually) the right hand and to transfer the pain to another part of the body by touching it with that hand. If desired, suggestions can also be made for a reduction of the pain in the new location. An instruction such as the following could be used:

> You can slowly allow your right hand to move so that it touches your back at the most painful spot. . . . As it touches your back, you can be aware of the painful sensations flowing from your back into your hand. . . . Now slowly allow your hand to move toward your left shoulder, feeling the pain lessen as it does so. . . . As your hand touches your left shoulder, you can feel the pain move to your shoulder, but somewhat less than before. Now remove your hand and let it slowly drop to your lap, relaxing as it goes.

Pain can also be transformed into other sensations, and this procedure is likewise useful in cases of chronic, psychogenic pain. In addition, the signaling function of pain is retained, while the suffering and incapacitation associated with it are reduced. For example, suggestions can be given that the individual will experience an itching, tingling, or warm sensation in the place of and at the site of the pain rather than the pain itself. To some extent, this technique is based on the common observation that the label we attach to something might in part determine how we respond to it (a rose by another name might *not* smell as sweet), because the meaning of an event or object is partly a function of its name. For example, we might respond quite

HMA-F

differently to a behavior labeled *aggressive* than to one labeled *forthright*, although the actual behavior could be the same in both cases. The client might be instructed as follows:

> As you pay close attention to the sensations in your back (the location of the pain), you can become aware of a feeling of warmth. As you continue to pay attention to this feeling of warmth, it will gradually replace all other feelings so that all you feel in that area is warmth. And you can allow that feeling of warmth to remain for as long as you have need of it.

## Hypnotic Analgesia and Anesthesia

Analgesia is defined as a dulling of sensation without loss of consciousness and is produced hypnotically by suggestions of numbness at the location of the pain. In hypnotic anesthesia, the individual experiences a loss of sensation. The same procedures are used to produce both phenomena. The difference is in how the client responds to the suggestions. High hypnotizables can experience anesthesia, whereas most individuals only experience analgesia. Anesthesia and analgesia can be accomplished in one of two ways. The client can be asked to imagine the painful area becoming numb directly, as if a shot of novocain had been given or an anesthetic lotion had been applied. Or suggestions could be given for one hand to become numb, and the numbness could then be transferred to the painful area. The latter technique involves an extra ritual, which might make it powerful in certain instances.

Because it involves teaching coping skills to clients, hypnotic analgesia can be useful for chronic pain, both intractable and progressive. Because it normally reduces pain, rather than eliminates it, hypnotic analgesia can also be effective for psychogenic pain, in which it is important to the individual that some pain sensations be retained. Clients can be put in charge of their pain reduction by instructions to keep only as much pain as they need at the present time, suggesting that they might wish to reduce it even further at some (unspecified) time in the future.

Analgesia and anesthesia can be taught as part of hypnotic-skills training (see chapter 2) or induced through Ericksonian procedures. Resistant clients, in particular those receiving secondary gain for their pain, might resist a skills-training approach in which they are taught how to induce analgesia and anesthesia, but they might be responsive to a more indirect method such as the following (embedded suggestions are printed in capital letters and are vocally stressed):

> As you focus your attention on your painful area, you CAN if you wish FEEL a gradual NUMBNESS in that area. As you continue to focus your attention, you can feel the numbness spread to all parts of the painful area, leaving MUCH LESS PAIN! And you can decide YOU DON'T NEED THAT PAIN and can allow yourself to FEEL LESS PAIN.

The hypnotic routine for transfer of analgesia proceeds similarly.

> You can feel your right hand becoming numb, so that it loses more and more feeling from the wrist on down. . . . Now slowly place that hand on the location of your pain and gradually allow the numbness to move from your hand to the painful area, feeling the NUMBNESS SPREAD as you do so. . . . And as the NUMBNESS SPREADS, you can KEEP only AS MUCH PAIN AS YOU NEED, and you can DECIDE YOURSELF WHEN YOU NO LONGER NEED YOUR PAIN. And you can KEEP just as much PAIN as YOU NEED right now until you NO LONGER NEED YOUR PAIN.

## Dissociative Techniques

There are a variety of ways in which clients can be helped via hypnosis to dissociate from painful sensations. In dissociation, individuals are helped to remove themselves from the direct experience of their pain. Whereas individuals with greater trance capacity gain most from these methods, most people are able to obtain some relief from them. Indeed, some people regularly experience such out-of-the-body experiences. One method, which is used in such minor surgery as dental work, consists of instructing subjects in a trance to imagine themselves detaching from their bodies and actually looking at themselves from the outside. If necessary, they can take themselves farther from their bodies. The "telescope technique" consists of instructing subjects in a trance to imagine their pain wrapped up in a bag and then viewed through the wrong end of an expanding telescope. As the pain becomes smaller and farther away, it also, because of the distancing effect, becomes less intense. Clients can also be told to take themselves on mental trips during painful procedures. This technique can be used with both acute and chronic pain, except where secondary gain is a prominent feature. The following routine might serve as an example:

> As you lie back in the [dental] chair, you can imagine yourself slowly floating away from your body and looking at it from above, near the ceiling. As you see yourself lying there, you can feel a sense of peace and detachment. You know that it is you, but you feel somehow separate, feeling nothing but peace. You watch what is going on with casual curiosity but no great involvement or interest. It is like it is happening to another person with whom you have no real involvement. And you know that you can recreate this experience any time you wish.

## Distraction Techniques

Hypnotic distraction takes advantage of the fact that we do not notice unpleasant or painful sensations when we are absorbed in pleasantly involving activities. The ability to lose oneself timelessly in certain activities or thoughts to the exclusion of other thoughts appears to be related to trance capacity, so that good subjects are likely to find these methods easier to perform. Most people can learn them to some extent, however. The subject is asked to visualize (hallucinate) a pleasant scene and then to concentrate on it and on the positive-feeling state it elicits. It is often not necessary, and might not even be desirable, for the client to describe the scene. This allows the client perfect freedom in choosing one. The hypnotherapist could choose a scene for the client but should ask which types of scenes the client enjoys, to avoid choosing one that might be upsetting. This methodology is appropriate for both acute and chronic pain clients, and it has the added advantage of teaching the individual a coping strategy. The client can practice this technique, using a variety of pleasant scenes, under the guidance of the hypnotherapist, who gradually withdraws from active involvement. The following routine might serve as an example:

> And as you lie there very relaxed [or in a trance], you can transport yourself to a very special place of your own choosing that has many happy associations for you. When you are there, please let me know by raising the index finger of your right hand. . . . Good! Now you can vividly feel yourself in that place, feeling all the pleasant feelings associated with being there. Feel how happy you are, how peaceful. Revel in the feelings. Absorb them into the innermost fibre of your being. Take a few minutes now to enjoy them to the exclusion of all other feelings and sensations. (Pause.) Now that you know how good it feels to be here, you can also know that you can come here any time you wish, in order to experience again these pleasant and wonderful feelings.

## Cognitive Restructuring

As mentioned earlier in the chapter, maladaptive thinking can interfere with an individual's ability to cope with pain. Negative thoughts such as "the pain will never go away" and "there's nothing I can do", are negative types of self-hypnosis that lead to helplessness and hopelessness (see chapter 3). These patterns of thought become self-fulfilling. The client becomes discouraged and gives up.

Catastrophic thinking such as "I can't stand this pain" and "if I'm too active the pain is going to keep on getting worse and worse until it's unbearable" can intensify pain and lead to avoidance. Instead of employing coping strategies such as self-hypnosis or activity as a distractor, the catastrophizer is passive, dwells on the pain, and magnifies it.

Clients who manifest these self-defeating patterns of thinking are often unable to benefit from hypnosis unless some type of cognitive restructuring is employed. Several cognitive-restructuring procedures are described in detail in the chapter on depression. For pain control, the most useful cognitive-restructuring technique is the two-column method. First, the therapist helps the client identify self-defeating thoughts. These negative thoughts are frequently verbalized aloud by the client in the form of complaints or objections to the treatment procedures. For example, Margaret, who suffered from chronic lower-back pain, complained constantly about how she couldn't bear the pain, that it would "surely kill" her, that she couldn't do anything except stay in bed because every movement was "like torture." Furthermore, she made her condition worse by resisting the instructions of her physical therapist to exercise.

Margaret sought hypnosis as a last resort. The hypnotherapist (W. G.) explained to Margaret how her negative thinking was a type of negative self-hypnosis (Araoz, 1981, 1982, 1985) and now, for her to get better, she would have to learn to modify these thoughts. She was told how hypnosis could be used to control self-defeating patterns of thinking.

The first step was to help Margaret identify her maladaptive thoughts. A self-monitoring form was used for this purpose (Table 5.2). The therapist also pointed out her negative self-defeating thoughts when she verbalized them. Next she and the hypnotherapist collaborated to construct therapeutic suggestions that could counteract the effect of her negative thinking (see Table 5.2). These therapeutic suggestions later served as hypnotic suggestions during hetero- and self-hypnosis. In addition, Margaret was taught to use relaxation procedures and hypnotic analgesia for pain relief.

## CASE EXAMPLE

Brian's case will now be presented as an example of pain management through hypnotherapy. Brian was referred to one of the authors (W. G.) by his physician for treatment of lower-back pain, ulcers, insomnia and anxiety. The physician was treating and monitoring the ulcers medically. However, he recognized that Brian was in need of psychological, as well as medical, treatment.

Brian's treatment, like that of most of our clients, was multifaceted. We find a broad-spectrum approach to be particularly important in cases of

Table 5.2. Sample Two-Column Method

| Negative Thoughts | Therapeutic Suggestions |
|---|---|
| 1. I can't stand the pain; it's going to kill me. | 1. I may not like the pain. It's unpleasant, but it won't kill me. |
| 2. I have to stay in bed. It hurts too much to do anything. Every movement is like torture. | 2. Getting out of bed is therapeutic. Eventually I'll feel better if I spend less time in bed. |
| 3. Exercise will just make my pain worse. | 3. Exercise will eventually make me feel better. |
| 4. It's hopeless; I'll never get better. There's nothing I can do to get better. | 4. There is hope. I will get better. All I have to do is use my techniques and keep active. |

psychogenic pain. Brian was very interested in hypnosis and proved to be an excellent subject. Symptom relief of pain was obtained through hypnotic analgesia. Brian was responsive to direct suggestions to feel numb. Following a relaxation induction, it was suggested that Brian's fingers and hands would start to feel numb in response to the cue "numb out" and that the numbness would spread throughout his body to his back and his stomach. He experienced dissociation in response to the suggestion that he would allow his mind to drift off to some pleasant place and that he would feel as though his mind were leaving his body. For his insomnia, it was suggested that he would become so comfortable and relaxed that he would drift off into a natural sleep. These suggestions were recorded on a cassette that Brian was instructed to use only at night to sleep and at other times only when the pain became extreme. These instructions were given so as to avoid masking pain that might be serving as a warning signal or that could be used to direct Brian's attention to the sources of his anxiety.

Treatment was also directed toward the source of Brian's symptoms. He was instructed to use pain for biofeedback, as a signal from his body that could be used to identify what it was that bothered him.

Brian employed the self-monitoring form described earlier in the chapter (see p. 63) and found that his ulcer attacks, back pain, and insomnia were mainly in response to on-the-job-stress. Brian's boss was extremely critical and demanding and threw frequent temper tantrums, screaming at his employees. Brian's symptoms occurred at work or night while he was lying in bed worrying about his job. Several times he had left work because he had been "sick." Just prior to his beginning treatment, Brian had begun to call in sick in the mornings on a fairly regular basis. He nearly always felt better when away from work. This relationship became clear to him, and he was receptive to considering such alternatives as looking for a different job, being more assertive with his boss, and learning to handle stress more effectively.

Brian was taught self-hypnosis and was instructed to practice it for the purpose of reducing anxiety. Hypnotic desensitization (see chapter 4) was also employed. As part of the desensitization, Brian was asked to imagine himself coping with anxiety-provoking situations such as his boss's criticizing and yelling at him, speaking up to his boss when his rights were being violated, and going to interviews for new job positions.

In addition, the concept of secondary gain was explained to Brian, and he was advised not to use his pain as an excuse for being absent from work. He agreed to begin using the techniques he was learning instead. Brian continued to be monitored by his physician, who instructed him to follow a diet program as treatment for the ulcer. With this multifaceted program, Brian became symptom free within 6 weeks and eventually found more acceptable employment.

## SUMMARY

This chapter has described the multifaceted nature of the phenomenon we call pain. It has presented ways of assessing the experience of pain and discussed both general and specific considerations and techniques in the treatment of pain. The type of pain for which each technique might be most useful was also described. Where possible, examples of actual hypnotic routines were presented. Because pain is such a complex phenomenon, including cognitive, behavioral, and emotional aspects, it is important that treatment programs likewise be multifaceted in nature, to insure maintenance of therapeutic gains. The case example illustrates both this approach and the use of self-hypnosis as a coping strategy.

# Chapter 6

# Habit Disorders

Perhaps the most sought after treatment for the common habit disorders of smoking and overeating is hypnosis. The appeal of hypnosis for these difficult problems seems to arise from its perceived promise of a quick and painless cure.

The traditional hypnotic approach to controlling eating and smoking involves direct suggestion. For example, the hypnotist might say "Your desire to smoke will completely disappear." A review of the controlled studies of traditional hypnosis treatments (Wadden & Anderton, 1982) concluded that traditional methods alone are not notably effective for smoking and eating control.

On the other hand, cognitive–behavioral hypnotherapy, representing an integration of cognitive–behavioral therapy and hypnotic techniques, has shown encouraging results in overcoming cigarette addiction. Two of the authors (Golden & Friedberg, 1986), using a multiple-case-study format, found that 8 out of 12 clients (67%) stopped smoking for at least 4 weeks after completion of a four-session cognitive–behavioral hypnotic treatment (see the case example in the last section of this chapter). After a 1-year follow-up interval, 7 out of 12 (58%) remained abstinent. Also, nine smoking clients were treated with an abbreviated one-session version of this CBH procedure. Five out of 5 (56%) stopped smoking for at least 4 weeks following treatment, and 43% (4 out of 9) remained nonsmoking at a 1-year follow-up.

In our use of hypnosis for habit disorders, we focus on helping clients modify their behavior and the patterns of thinking that lead to and maintain their addictions. We have found cognitive–behavioral hypnotherapy to be effective in treating overeating and smoking. The treatments we apply to these habit disorders include self-monitoring, cognitive restructuring, imaginal rehearsal, thought stopping, and self-hypnosis. We also incorporate behavior modification principles for habit control, such as positive reinforcement.

# ASSESSMENT OF HABIT
# DISORDERS

The first step in our treatment involves identifying the antecedents that lead to overeating and smoking. The client might be directed to self-monitor his or her patterns by keeping a log of the time, place, activity, and thoughts and feelings experienced before and during eating or smoking. The therapist and client then review the written record and identify the cognitive, emotional, and situational antecedents associated with the problematic habit (Table 6.1). Applying another technique, *evocative imagery*, the client vividly imagines an eating or smoking situation and then identifies the thoughts and feelings produced by the imagery that control the problem behavior.

Once they are identified, we can subdivide the negative thoughts that maintain habit disorders into three categories: (a) low frustration tolerance, (b) self-condemnation, and (c) excuses.

Low frustration tolerance includes thoughts that exaggerate the discomfort and effort required to overcome the habit and thoughts that minimize the ability of the individual to cope with the stress and discomfort that can lead to habit indulgence. Thoughts such as "It's too tempting to resist" or "I've got to have a cigarette" imply that the individual is too weak to avoid eating or smoking, because the effort involved is just too great. Similarly, self-defeating thoughts such as "I'm so depressed, I have to eat" or "I'm so uptight, I need a cigarette "also imply that the discomfort of a negative feeling requires eating or smoking.

Self-condemnation involves berating oneself for having the bad habit; for example, "I keep smoking. What's wrong with me?" The individual then labels himself or herself "weak," "inadequate," or "worthless." Such self-condemning thoughts often create feelings of hopelessness or despair, which only encourages continuation of the problem.

Finally, excuses are self-defeating thoughts whereby the client fools himself or herself into justifying overeating or smoking; for example, "I'll just have one slice of cake" or "I'll stop tomorrow."

All of these negative thoughts are self-suggestions that interfere with an individual's ability to resist habit cravings.

# SITUATIONAL FACTORS

Perhaps the most important situational factor that leads to overeating or smoking is the *availability* of food or cigarettes. Food and cigarettes are more likely to trigger habit indulgence if they (a) are in one's possession, rather than one's having to go out and buy them; (b) are openly exposed, rather than

Table 6.1. Sample Eating Log of Weight-Reduction Client

| DAY/TIME | FOOD & AMOUNT | ACTIVITY | LOCATION | THOUGHTS | FEELINGS |
|---|---|---|---|---|---|
| Mon. 8:30a.m. | 1½ bagels, 2 tbs cream cheese, coffee/milk | Reading | Kitchen | I should go on a diet. My husband is so thoughtless! | Annoyed; angry at husband |
| 1:00p.m. | 1 peanut butter & jelly sandwich, 1 glass milk | Reading | Kitchen | Thinking about kids | Stressed; fatigued |
| 6:p.m. | ½ cup macaroni & cheese, 1 cup diet coke, 3 chocolate chip cookies | Talking with family | Kitchen | Thinking about chores | Starved |
| 9.30p.m. | 6 chocolate chip cookies | Watching TV | Den | Do I really want these cookies? | Bored. |

stored or hidden; or (c) require little effort to prepare. Also, the *range* of permissible eating or smoking situations can influence the habit. The more situations there are in which one is permitted to eat or smoke, the more likely it is that consumption will occur.

Once the negative, habit-sustaining thoughts and feelings are uncovered, the techniques to be discussed next can be applied to replace them.

# TREATMENT TECHNIQUES

## Cognitive Restructuring

One method of cognitive restructuring that is particularly useful in habit modification is the two-column method (see also chapter 3, 4 and 5). Its use in habit control is illustrated with a weight-loss client, Ursula.

The client and the therapist (W. G.) worked together to pinpoint the negative thoughts or self-suggestions that led to overeating and then jointly formulated constructive suggestions for hetero- and self-hypnosis to neutralize her self-defeating thoughts. The negative self-suggestions were identified through self-monitoring and evocative imagery. Problematic situations for Ursula included walking past fast food restaurants such as pizzerias or staying home alone while feeling lonely and frustrated. Ursula's negative thoughts and therapeutic suggestions, using the two-column method, are reproduced in Table 6.2.

## Imaginal Rehearsal

Imaginal rehearsal is a procedure wherein the client mentally practices succeeding at his or her efforts to control eating, smoking, or other problem behaviors. Imaginal rehearsal can be applied to eating and smoking control in these ways: (a) preparation for the situations, thoughts and feelings that lead to smoking and overeating and mental rehearsal of various coping techniques for maintaining self-control, (b) prevention of setbacks or relapses.

*Preparation for eating or smoking situations.* As the therapist reviews the client's smoking or eating record, specific situations, thoughts, or feelings are identified that trigger the bad habit (see Table 6.1 for examples). Once the client learns the techniques of cognitive restructuring, behavior modification, and self-hypnosis, he or she can practice these skills mentally and then be better prepared to implement them in the actual situations.

For weight control, imaginal rehearsal is an effective preparation for controlled daily eating, because it programs the client to eat sensibly and not succumb to whims and impulses. Initially, an individualized, moderate daily

1Table 6.2. Sample Two-Column Method

| Negative Thoughts | Therapeutic Suggestions |
|---|---|
| 1. What difference does it make if I eat or not? | 1. It makes a difference. I want to achieve my goals to look better, be healthier, feel better and be able to fit into a size 10 dress. (Also use the image of fitting into a size 10 dress) |
| 2. I can eat what I want today; I just won't eat tomorrow. | 2. It's an excuse. It doesn't work that way. When I do try to starve myself the next day, I end up breaking down and eating more. I can eat whatever I want, just in moderation, and reach my goal. |
| 3. I'll never succeed, I'll never reach my goal, I'll never be thin again. | 3. If I say never, I never will. I did it before and I can do it again. |
| 4. (When feeling lonely). I can't stand feeling lonely. I've just got to do something to stop this feeling. I just have to eat. | 4. To reduce loneliness, I can join activities and find outlets other than food. But just the same, I'll probably feel lonely at times and, when I do, I don't have to suppress it with food. I can use the feelings of loneliness to motivate myself to do something constructive. |
| 5. (When frustrated), I can't stand feeling frustrated. | 5. It's okay to be frustrated. It can be a time to do some problem solving. |
| 6. I hate myself for being so fat (low self-esteem). | 6. Even if I'm overweight, I can still accept myself. Being overweight does not make me less worthwhile as a person. |
| 7. No one will like me this way. I can't stand to be rejected (social anxiety). | 7. Some men don't care whether or not I'm overweight. They still seem interested. Women don't seem to care at all. But even if I do get rejected, I can take it and accept myself anyway. And it's better to be out than staying home and eating. |

eating schedule is formulated, based on the client's eating record. The client is then hypnotized and guided in imagination through the daily eating schedule. The imagery can include eating only planned meals or snacks, ordering or preparing reasonable portions of food, avoiding or resisting temptations, and ultimately succeeding.

The therapist can reinforce imaginal rehearsal by asking the client to imagine the positive results of his or her efforts. The client imagines himself or herself as a thinner person who looks and feels better. The image is adjusted as lower weights are achieved, so that the client's anticipated self-picture is 5 or 10 lbs thinner than his or her present weight.

For home practice, the client uses imaginal rehearsal each day before eating begins. An example of a therapist-directed imaginal rehearsal for eating control would be (after a hypnotic induction):

Feeling so relaxed, comfortable, and receptive to suggestions, you can imagine yourself planning your day. Yes, planning what you will eat and how much you will eat. You know what the plan is, and now you will see yourself carrying it out fully, correctly, the way you want it to be. Starting with your shopping, only from the prepared list; yes, shopping for these healthy items on the list. And you walk past junk foods. Next, taking the food home, storing the food away, putting all snack foods out of sight.

Now, you begin with the morning meal, seeing the entire meal, the portions, the kinds of food, according to your plan. Seeing yourself resisting temptations so successfully. You proceed through the morning with no additional eating. . . . Now visualizing lunch. Feeling a sense of relaxed confidence that you will eat according to the plan.

The script continues until the day's eating is visualized. Imaginal rehearsal, of course, should be tailored to the needs of the client; for instance, it might be necessary for specific meals or special events only, rather than for every meal.

*Prevention of relapses.* The relapse, or setback, is a major obstacle to long-term smoking cessation and weight control. The old, destructive habit usually "reasserts" itself from time to time, threatening to undo the client's hard-earned progress. Of course, the client is ultimately responsible for relapses. Although setbacks are a common occurrence in habit change, it is important to minimize their effects and reduce the likelihood of a sustained relapse. Imaginal rehearsal can prepare the client for potential setbacks and relapses.

Perhaps the key feature of relapse prevention is therapist *anticipation* of the possibility, so that he or she can help the client to cope with it. Using imaginal rehearsal, the therapist prepares the client for setbacks that might occur. The client can then picture the specific cues, situational, emotional and cognitive, that might trigger a setback and imagine getting through these rough spots without habit indulgence. For instance, Gene (a client of F. F.) initially stopped smoking but was concerned about temptations to light up after meals or when feeling nervous. The following suggestions for relapse prevention were given to Gene:

Now you can anticipate the possibility of slipping; yes, anticipate the possibility. You anticipate the situations, the feelings, and the thoughts that could lead to smoking: situations such as after meals and feelings such as nervousness. These have been smoking triggers. Now you imagine drinking your coffee after dinner, and you feel tempted to light up. But you are in control. Yes, you tell yourself that you can enjoy your coffee without smoking. Yes, without smoking. And you see yourself succeeding, giving yourself credit for resisting.

Furthermore, Gene was prepared for the possibility of an actual setback with the following script:

And you understand that, as a human being, you might have setbacks. You might have none. But if you should slip and smoke, you will minimize the setback. Now imagine . . . smoking in response to a stressful day at work, thinking to yourself "just one can't hurt." You have now smoked the cigarette.

It is done. But you will stop the setback right now. Yes, shorten the setback as much as possible by thinking to yourself that smoking cessation is not all or none. You will stop the setback and reassert your control. Yes, stop the setback, reassert your control, and feel good. You will use all of your well-learned coping skills — relaxation, breathing, self-hypnosis — you can do it: Stop the setback and master the habit. Returning to those feelings of self-control.

## Thought Stopping

A significant number of clients with habit problems, especially heavy smokers and overeaters, think about their habits much of the time. If one's mental activity is almost continuously absorbed in thinking about or imagining eating or smoking, then the pressure to indulge in the habit can become overwhelming. It is likely that such an obsessive thought pattern could become a source of emotional stress or frustration, with thoughts of tempting foods or the next smoke.

*Thought stopping* is a technique for interrupting such obsessive thinking patterns and giving the client a greater sense of control over her or his habit. The following steps can be used to teach the technique:

1. Ask the client to verbalize the habit-related thoughts and images such as imagining the smell and taste of some high-calorie food and thinking "I can't control myself. I've just got to have some." As the client verbalizes these thoughts, the therapist says "stop" in a loud, abrupt manner. This is then repeated.
2. Ask the client to think the self-defeating thoughts, rather than to verbalize them. The therapist again commands "stop" at a random interval. This is then repeated.
3. Tell the client to substitute a constructive, pleasant, or relaxing self-suggestion after the stop signal, such as "I can control my habit."
4. Finally, the client is asked to think the self-defeating thoughts, to vigorously command "stop" in his or her thinking (silently), and to substitute the constructive thoughts and suggestions.

In one case, Laura reported a nearly constant stream of thoughts about eating. The thought-stopping technique was taught as described. Then, she substituted pleasant sexual thoughts about intimacy with her husband after the command to stop. With home practice, she reported a dramatic reduction in food-related thoughts and an increase in feelings of well-being.

## Self-Hypnosis

Self-hypnosis can be used to control anxiety, to facilitate cognitive restructuring, to reduce cravings for nicotine and food, to create pleasant feelings of well-being that deter habit indulgence, and for imaginal rehearsal.

In addition to minimizing the discomforts involved in habit removal, self-hypnosis can help the client focus on the highly rewarding aspects of self-control. To create these positive feelings, self-hypnotic suggestions can be constructed emphasizing self-praise for successes and the reasons for self-change: to live longer, be healthier, and feel and look better. A sample self-hypnotic script for smoking cessation might be phrased as follows:

> Now I will focus on my goal: to be free of smoking, yes, to be totally free of the smoking habit. Imagine that sense of freedom; I am no longer a slave to the smoking habit. No longer am I ruled by the habit. I am taking control; I will put that bad habit behind me. Yes, I will put it behind me because I have that control. I have that control because I don't need cigarettes anymore.
>
> Now, for every cigarette resisted, for each cigarette I don't smoke, I will give myself credit. Yes, I will give myself credit for every cigarette resisted, because I have that control. Every time I praise myself for resisting, I will be more powerfully motivated to continue; I will be powerfully motivated, and I will feel better, so much better, knowing that I am taking control.

Self-hypnosis can also promote feelings of self-confidence and self-acceptance. Here is an example of a self-hypnosis script designed to replace self-condemning thoughts:

> Now I begin to focus so intently on myself in a positive, confident way. I suspend all judgments of myself. Yes, suspend them. I see myself as a person, a human being, no more, no less. And I realize that no single word or phrase describes me, no single phrase. There are many images of myself, and I will focus on strengthening myself, yes, strengthening, rather than condemning. Building psychological strength — no longer condemning — it only hurts me. I will proceed without judgements, and evaluate whatever I do for what it is; yes, evaluate my actions, not myself.

## CASE EXAMPLE

As an illustration of modern hypnotherapy for habit disorders, we will describe our four-session program for smoking cessation as applied to a particular case, Sally. This somewhat standardized approach reflects an integration of cognitive–behavioral procedures and hypnosis.

### Session 1

The therapist (W. G.) initially explained how hypnotherapeutic techniques could be effective in stopping smoking. Then Sally's misunderstandings about hypnosis, such as her hope for a dramatic and painless resolution to her smoking problem, were noted and corrected. The therapist explained that successful hypnosis required her active involvement if her goal were to be achieved.

Initially, Sally's smoking history was taken, and she identified some of the current circumstances that were associated with smoking. To clarify the major smoking antecedents, she was assigned a smoking record to monitor frequency of smoking, places where she smoked, and thoughts and feelings experienced before each cigarette. The therapist reviewed her reasons for wanting to quit, so that all negatively phrased motivators such as "I don't want to die of cancer" were reworded in a positive way; for example, "I want to live longer; I want to be healthier." In subsequent sessions, motivational suggestions were based on her reasons for wanting to stop smoking. In general, most hypnotists formulate suggestions with positive phrasing.

Finally, Sally received hypnotic skills training (as explained in chapter 2). She was most receptive to the hand-lightness and hand-levitation exercise, which she then practiced at home.

## Session 2

The second session began with a review of the client's smoking record, which uncovered these specific smoking triggers: job stress, interpersonal anxiety, boredom, and frustration. The types of thinking that led to smoking included perfectionist demands and thoughts reflecting low tolerance of discomfort: "I can't stand feeling tense; I've got to have a cigarette." Alternative thoughts and behaviors for each smoking situation were developed. For instance, the smoking trigger "I've just got to have a cigarette" was replaced with the positive hypnotic suggestion "I will have more and more control over my desire to smoke as I learn to relax." In addition, self-relaxation methods were advised as a healthier way to reduce anxiety, stress, and cravings.

Next, a hypnotic induction was given using hand levitation, the hypnotic-skills strategy that was previously most effective with Sally. Relaxation instructions were also interspersed during the induction procedure by suggesting that Sally attend to her breathing and allow it to slow down and deepen. Suggestions of "relaxation flowing through her body" were also given.

To increase her relaxed feelings, Sally was guided through a pleasant imaginal scene that had been developed in session before the induction. Following the initial hypnosis, she was shown how to induce self-hypnosis by taking five long, slow, deep breaths while experiencing an emerging sense of relaxation with each exhalation. Furthermore, hypnotic suggestions were given that she would be able to delay smoking on impulse. During the delay she was asked to focus on breathing and other self-hypnotic devices to alleviate anxiety and cravings for nicotine.

Sally's next home assignment was to continue logging each cigarette smoked but to delay smoking for 15 minutes after the onset of a craving and induce self-hypnosis during the interval. The delay time impresses upon the client that he or she does not have to smoke in response to a smoking urge or stress. The sense of self-control is further reinforced if the client chooses not to smoke after the delay interval.

## Session 3

Sally's smoking record was again reviewed during the third session, and her successful smoking delays were verbally praised. The therapist requested a detailed review of all methods used by the client that effectively subdued anxiety and the cravings for nicotine. Areas of difficulty were evaluated, and new strategies to deal with these problems were developed.

Then, the induction technique of session 2 was used to hypnotize the client. While hypnotized, the therapist suggested that Sally visualize herself in each smoking situation and imagine herself coping successfully in each situation.

Following hypnosis, Sally proposed a specific date to stop smoking, and the therapist offered her the alternative of cutting back smoking frequency gradually or all at once. Sally chose immediate cessation, which, according to the therapist's instruction, would begin 24 hours prior to the final session. The cessation of smoking before termination permits the therapist to pinpoint the client's coping problems as they are occurring.

## Session 4

Similar to many clients treated with this four-session protocol, Sally reported feelings of discomfort at the fourth session, arising from the 24 hours of nicotine deprivation.

Following a hypnotic induction via hand levitation and relaxation suggestions, the therapist restated Sally's reasons for quitting the cigarette habit. Next, Sally was instructed to imagine herself in smoking situations, and, whenever the visualization produced stress or cravings, she was to signal by lifting her right index finger. The therapist then directed her to reduce stress and cravings with the previously taught cognitive, behavioral, and hypnotic techniques and finally to lower her finger when she succeeded.

Lastly, to cope effectively with the possibility of posttreatment setbacks, she imagined herself "slipping" and *not* giving up by suggesting to herself "A slip is not failure. I am still progressing and *can* control my smoking. I *will* continue to succeed." Also, Sally imagined circumstances where cravings could not be controlled. Effective coping with such high levels of discomfort involved self-directed thoughts such as "the cravings will pass; I *can* get through this discomfort without smoking."

Six months after terminating the four-session treatment, Sally reported successful and complete abstinence from smoking. Significantly, she concluded that hypnosis was a powerful coping skill, rather than the magic cure that she had originally sought.

## SUMMARY

Cognitive–behavioral hypnotherapy can be an effective intervention for smoking and overeating. The therapeutic goal is replacement of habit-sustaining attitudes with positive and healthy thoughts and behavior.

Within the cognitive–behavioral approach, the hypnotherapist is armed with a variety of techniques that can be tailored to the client's preferences. Using these methods, the client quickly learns how effective, long-term control of the habit problem can be achieved.

# Chapter 7

# Treatment of Sexual Dysfunction

In this chapter we will show how hypnosis can be therapeutically applied to sexual dysfunction and sexual deviations. In overview, hypnosis in sex therapy can be used (a) as a diagnostic tool to uncover etiologic and maintaining factors, (b) to administer general suggestions for self-confidence and self-esteem, (c) to reduce sexual performance anxiety, (d) to suggest direct removal of symptoms, (e) to work through emotional conflicts, (f) to alter sexual preferences, and (g) to increase and decrease sexual desire (modified from Crasilneck & Hall, 1985).

## INTEGRATING HYPNOSIS WITH TRADITIONAL SEX THERAPY

The physiological mechanisms that mediate sexual desire, arousal, and orgasm can be easily disrupted by anxiety and stress. Briefly stated, the purpose of sex therapy is to reduce or remove emotional blocks that interfere with sexual responsiveness. Hypnosis in sex therapy has a special capacity to create and reinforce erotic thoughts and imagery.

Traditional sex therapists, following the lead of Masters and Johnson (1970), prescribe a primarily behavioral approach: Couples are directed to proceed gradually from nonsexual touching and pleasuring to more intimate encounters that culminate in intercourse. Despite the success of Masters and Johnson's techniques, several limitations to their methods are apparent: (a) an understanding and cooperative sexual partner must be available; (b) the couple must set aside several home sessions per week to practice therapeutic exercises; (c) disorders of sexual desire were not treated; (d) one condition in particular, erectile dysfunction, showed a high failure rate in the original Masters and Johnson treatment program; (e) couples exhibiting psychopathology in addition to the presented sexual problem were excluded from treatment. Therefore, the applicability of traditional sex therapy to couples showing more general problems remains untested.

Finally, Masters and Johnson did not examine the role of fantasies and imagery in causing, as well as overcoming, sexual problems. In our opinion, their neglect of imagery factors imposed limitations on their approach. Specifically, some sexual problems stem from a lack of sexual imagery or are the result of negative images that interfere with sexual responsiveness. Other conditions are due to negative emotional reactions to sexual images. For instance, a number of our clients have reported extreme guilt about their need to employ various fantasies to get sexually aroused with their spouses. Once the guilt was removed, they were able to enjoy sex with their spouses.

Integrating modern hypnosis with traditional sex therapy can assist the therapist in overcoming such limitations. Hypnotherapy allows the clinician to identify and directly alter the maladaptive attitudes and beliefs underlying the dysfunctional behavior. Furthermore, sex hypnotherapy can be effective even if a sexual partner is unavailable or uncooperative. We have found hypnosis to be especially valuable in treating single individuals who suffer from sexual performance anxiety. Because a regular partner is not available, they cannot employ traditional sex therapy techniques such as sensate focus (nondemand touching and caressing) for the purposes of anxiety reduction. On the other hand, hypnosis and self-hypnosis can be successfully used with such individuals.

Araoz (1982) has pointed out that hypnosis is probably the treatment of choice for desire disorders. According to Kaplan (1979), these clients engage in a "turnoff" phenomenon by attending to negative thoughts about their partners, such as focusing on their partners' negative traits, and thereby suppressing desire. Araoz (1982) considered this sexual turnoff to be another example of negative self-hypnosis. Hypnosis is particularly appropriate as a treatment for desire problems, because more sexually positive thoughts and images can be substituted for negative ones. Of course, the reasons (if any) for the negative thinking, such as anger and resentment, need to be explored too.

In keeping with an individualized approach, hypnotherapy for sexual problems would be indicated for clients (a) who request it, (b) who are receptive when it is presented by the clinician, (c) who are chronically anxious or anxious in sexual situations, and (d) with negative or no sexual imagery. Hypnosis is a powerful anti-anxiety agent that is most effective for sexual problems mediated by anxiety. For clients who reject "hypnosis" yet are receptive to "relaxation," the therapist can change the labeling of a hypnotic procedure to *relaxation training, self-control relaxation,* or a similar innocuous-sounding term.

# ETIOLOGICAL FACTORS

For the hypnotherapist, etiological factors in sexual dysfunction can be pinpointed by looking at negative thinking and imagery as well as sexually traumatic events in the client's background. For more detailed information, we refer the reader to Masters and Johnson's (1970) research into the histories of individuals with various sexual dysfunctions.

## Myths And Poor Sex Education

Despite the openness of discussion about sexual matters that began in the 1950s and 1960s and the enormous increase in scientifically based sexual information, competent and thorough sex education in our schools is available to only a minority of students. As a result of poor sex education, the constant flow of sex misinformation among adolescents and adults, and sensationalized sexual presentations in movies, fiction, and other media, many sexual myths prevail in our society.

Myths that a client might believe and that could interfere with sexual functioning include

1. Men should be able to attain an erection and satisfy their partners regardless of desire, mood, fatigue, or other obstacles.
2. Women must experience high-intensity multiple orgasms during sex or they are lacking.
3. Sex should be experienced several times a week in spite of busy schedules, early rising hours, and consequent fatigue.
4. Each new release of information about human sexuality should be viewed as yet another obligation to experience something new, for example, the erotic potential of the G Spot.

## Dyadic Factors

Two individuals who are capable of adequate sexual functioning could nevertheless show sexual difficulties as a couple. The couple-based causes of sexual disharmony include

1. Large differences between partners in desire for sexual contact
2. Partner incompatibility whereby one or both partners find each other physically or psychologically unattractive, or both
3. Unfulfilled expectations about not getting what one or both partners want overall in the relationship
4. Ambivalence about intimacy and commitment

5. Poor communication about sexual needs

6. Incompatible sexual preferences, such as one partner's wanting oral sex, and the other's not

7. Sexual sabotage, in which one partner tries to thwart sexual intimacy, such as by making excuses for not having sex

It is usually preferable to treat both partners when the sexual problem is a result of couple interaction. However, at times, the therapist might need to concentrate on one member of the relationship. Sometimes this can be done in the presence of the mate; at other times it is preferable to work with one member during the privacy of an individual session. Of course, clinical judgement is important in making these decisions. Care must be taken not to single out one partner as the cause of the problem. Even if the therapist does not think or say that one partner is the cause, a client might still get defensive. Therefore, when hypnosis is used as an adjunct to couples counseling, consider the alternatives of using it with both partners simultaneously or using it with one partner at a time in the presence of the other.

## Physiological or Psychological?

Although many, if not most, sexual dysfunctions are psychologically based, it is important to rule out physical factors. Physical factors that can result in sexual dysfunction include early diabetes, narcotic or alcohol abuse, genital disease (for example, urethritis), and neurological disorders (see Kaplan, 1983, for a more complete discussion of physical causes).

In general, the nonmedical hypnotherapist can reasonably conclude that a sexual dysfunction is (primarily) psychogenic if (a) there is a clearly established pattern of sexual difficulty in selected situations only, for instance, with one partner only or when a client is capable of sexual responsiveness through masturbation but not with a partner; (b) the onset of the client's dysfunction can be traced to a specific stressor or trauma, such as rape, that would be sufficient to partly or totally inhibit sexual functioning, including masturbation; (c) global sexual symptoms are secondary to such other emotional disturbances as schizophrenia or depression.

In the absence of emotional stress or trauma, the clinician is strongly advised to refer the client for a thorough medical screening to identify possible organic pathology related to sexual symptoms.

## ASSESSMENT OF SEXUAL DYSFUNCTION

It is important to assess not only the specific sexual dysfunction but also the individual's emotional reaction to it. If a client reports high levels of distress about his or her sexual behavior, then part of the problem (or perhaps the entire problem) is the client's evaluation of his or her behavior. For example, many of the female clients we have seen have reported anxiety or depressed feelings because they rarely attain orgasm during intercourse. Because infrequent occurrence of orgasms during intercourse is not unusual among women, the woman's *evaluation* of her sexual response is more the problem than the sexual response itself.

In contrast, nonnormative sexual behavior, such as a very low frequency of sexual intercourse in a marital relationship, if not accompanied by partner distress, would not fall into a "problem" category. Of course, if the individual's sexual behavior is hurtful or destructive to others, as in pedophilia, the clinician *and* society may then define the behavior as a problem.

Thus, it is imperative that the therapist determine the client's evaluation of his or her sexual behavior. Is it a source of distress? Hypnosis can be used to replace negative attitudes and evaluations with alternative views that lead to a more satisfactory sexual adjustment.

## Differential Diagnosis

*Triphasic concept of sexuality.* We find it useful to separate the sexual-response cycle into three phases (see Kaplan, 1979): desire, arousal, and orgasm. We prefer to define these phases in terms of behavioral measures or subjective reports that are easily understood by both therapist and client. *Desire* involves feelings of longing for sexual contact and intimacy. Sexual *arousal* is evidenced in the physical manifestations of penile erection in men and vaginal lubrication in women. Finally, *orgasm* in men involves sensations of orgasm immediately prior to and during an observable ejaculation. In women, a subjective experience of intense sexual pleasure and release, distinct from arousal, defines orgasm. Sexual dysfunction involves disruption in the progression of one or more of these phases. Table 7.1 outlines the major psychogenic sexual dysfunctions, which are described next.

Table 7.1. Major Psychogenic Sexual Dysfunctions

|  | Men | Women |
|---|---|---|
| *Desire* | Lack of desire | Lack of desire |
| *Arousal* | Erectile dysfunction | Failure of vaginal lubrication<br>Vaginismus<br>(severe contraction of vaginal muscles) |
| *Orgasm* | Premature or fast ejaculation | No prior orgasms (primary orgasmic dysfunction) |
|  | Delayed ejaculation or failure to ejaculate (ejaculatory incompetence) | Selective orgasmic inhibition |

*Male sexual dysfunctions.* For men reporting an *absence of sexual desire*, factors that might create the sexual turnoff include (a) insufficient levels of erotic thinking and imagery, (b) specific negative thoughts and feelings toward one's partner, (c) states of depression, and (d) intense performance anxiety that interferes with all phases of sexual response.

Lack of sexual arousal is manifested in erectile dysfunction, or, failure to attain or maintain an erection. Performance anxiety is the most common cause of psychogenic erectile difficulties. Other causes include thoughts and images of failing to perform sexually, self-doubt about sexual prowess and masculinity, fears of either partner disapproval or anger for sexual failure, guilt about sexual relations with others, or guilt about fantasies of sex with others during sexual contact.

A frequently reported male orgasmic problem is *premature ejaculation*, defined as male orgasm occurring before the man or his partner desires it. The principal causal factors in premature ejaculation are inability to recognize or control sexual sensations that signal orgasm, and anxiety about failing to please a sexual partner. Finally, the least common male sexual problem, delayed ejaculation, involves a sustained pattern of ejaculatory failure during intercourse.

*Female sexual dysfunctions.* The factors that produce *lack of sexual desire* in women are similar to those for the male. *Problems of sexual arousal*, manifested by absence of vaginal lubrication, are often the result of insufficient erotic stimulation or foreplay; performance anxiety, guilt, or shame about sexual contact; or anger toward the sexual partner.

A woman's reaction to insufficient foreplay can further complicate the problem. She might feel anxious about disapproval from her mate or fear that she will hurt his feelings. She might believe that she can not broach the issue with her partner because he will be *too* sensitive or threatened. Also, she might believe that she could not cope with his reactions of hurt or anger or that she might be responsible for *emasculating* him by expressing her sexual preferences.

Many women have *difficulty attaining orgasm* during intercourse. The pattern of stimulation required for female orgasm might not be reproducible during intercourse, regardless of therapeutic intervention. Therefore, intercourse might not be the most reliable way for a woman to achieve orgasm. So, we teach our anorgasmic female clients how to reach their orgasmic potential, and, when needed, help them to accept limited orgasmic response during coitus, without thinking of themselves as inadequate.

Factors that prevent female orgasm include (a) insufficient manual or oral stimulation (on average, women require 20 minutes of stimulation to induce orgasm); (b) maladaptive emotions, such as performance anxiety, fear of loss of control (perhaps fear of urinating or defecating), guilt about enjoying sex, and fear of disapproval for letting go and expressing sexual pleasure, by moaning for instance; and (c) negative self-suggestions that could be related to maladaptive emotions, including "I shouldn't enjoy sex" (guilt), or performance anxiety, including "I'm inadequate unless I achieve orgasm."

## TREATMENT TECHNIQUES FOR SEXUAL DYSFUNCTION

Treatment techniques that we find most effective for sexual dysfunction are evocative imagery, erotic imagery, hypnotic desensitization, cognitive restructuring, imaginal rehearsal, hypno-assertion, and, for modifying undesirable sexual preferences, aversive imagery.

### Evocative Imagery

Uncovering techniques such as evocative imagery during hypnosis can be used to identify negative thoughts that interfere with sexual desire, arousal, and orgasm. As Araoz (1982) has pointed out, one of the first steps in sex hypnotherapy is to make the client aware that these negative thoughts are a type of negative self-hypnosis causing the client to turn off sexually. One way of helping clients become aware of this negative self-hypnotic process is to have them imagine sexual encounters. Usually, the imagery evokes the negative thoughts and feelings that the client experiences in the real-life situation.

In the case of Sharon, who reported loss of sexual desire, evocative imagery was used to uncover the negative thoughts, attitudes, and feelings associated with sexual encounters with her fiancé:

*Therapist* (F.F.): All right, close your eyes and imagine you're in bed lying next to each other. Your fiancé starts putting his arms around you. Imagine his arms around you . . . . Now, what are you feeling?
*Sharon:* Tension, frustration.
*Therapist:* All right. And what are your thoughts?
*Sharon:* I *have* to please him. Also, I'm thinking of all the things I don't like about him. And I'd just rather not work on this.

The imagery revealed that Sharon was pressuring herself to please her partner, as well as focusing on his negative traits, which caused her to turn off. Sharon, reported having had a satisfying sexual relationship with her fiancé prior to their engagement. Her loss of sexual desire began as a result of her partner's continuing ambivalence about marrying her. Although he subsequently made the commitment, her sexual desire did not return. To reverse the client's sexual turnoff, erotic imagery was used.

## Erotic Imagery

In the technique of erotic imagery, the therapist encourages the client to create a series of personally appealing sexual fantasies that can replace negative thoughts and feelings. Erotic fantasies can be used by the client during masturbation and in real-life sexual encounters to (a) enhance sexual desire, (b) block anxiety-producing thoughts such as "I'll fail" that engender performance pressure, and (c) help trigger orgasms in men with delayed ejaculation or in women who have difficulty reaching orgasm. For the client reporting a dearth or absence of personal erotic imagery, the hypnotherapist can elicit from him or her prior sexual experiences that have produced the strongest sexual desire.

Positive client experiences with sexually oriented literature or movies should also be evaluated. The client who has limited experience with partners or sexually explicit material can be instructed to view tastefully presented sex education and therapy films (for example, Golden & Mills, 1982) or books (for example, Friday's (1973) book. Erotic sexual fantasies can be developed from this information and then suggested to the client under hypnosis. The goal is to produce sexual desire through erotic thoughts and fantasies that the client can repeat in the presence of a sexual partner. The client can also identify and focus on the positive physical traits and personality characteristics of the partner and use them to heighten sexual desire. The client can remind himself or herself about these traits during self-hypnosis and imagine becoming sexually desirous. The client can also be instructed to masturbate after this self-hypnosis practice.

Erotic imagery was used to help Sharon, the client with inhibited sexual desire previously described.

*Therapist:* Now that we've clarified how you are turning yourself off [by thinking you have to please your fiancé and focusing on his negative traits], let's use imagery to create the type of sexual situation you would enjoy.
*Sharon:* All right.
*Therapist:* Now, allow your eyes to close and feel comfortable. Imagine you and your male friend together. Just the way *you* want . . . imagine so vividly . . . the entire situation . . . feeling so serene, feeling comfortable, doing only what is comfortable, pleasing and sensual to you. . . . All right, slowly open your eyes. What did you imagine?
*Sharon:* I was lying in bed. We were talking to each other. There was an easy flow of conversation, a feeling of warmth, intimacy. I naturally began to touch him, to put my arms around him. It's slow and gradual. I am in control. That's what I like, my pace, rather than his grabbing and going too fast.

The client was asked to practice these erotic images during self-hypnosis for two 5-minute periods a day and then to *act out* the fantasy with her male friend. Furthermore, she imagined acting assertively to initiate the sexual encounter. In her words, "Let *me* do things to you sexually tonight." She did the home practice and reported a satisfying sexual encounter with her male friend where *she* took control.

## Hypnotic Desensitization

Sexual performance problems including erectile dysfunction, premature ejaculation, and arousal problems in women are often mediated by anxiety. Hypnotic desensitization, which has been described in chapter 4 for anxiety reduction, can likewise help clients overcome sexual performance anxiety. In applying desensitization to the treatment of sexual problems, the therapist and client begin by constructing a hierarchy that rank orders sexual or potentially sexual situations, ranging from the least to the most anxiety producing. Then the client is hypnotized and imaginally guided through each situation until he or she reports little or no anxiety from the presented scenes. Finally, the client is encouraged to approach the difficult sexual situations in real life.

In one case treated by W. G., Jim initially reported fast ejaculation. His girlfriend's criticism of his problem contributed to his developing a second problem, erectile dysfunction. The client's negative self-suggestions included demands and pressure to satisfy his girlfriend during intercourse and to live up to her high expectations for satisfaction. Putting such pressure on himself exacerbated his problem. Eventually, he was completely unable to attain an erection with his partner. At this point she left him, and he sought treatment.

Jim's erectile dysfunction and fast ejaculation were treated with a hypnotic desensitization procedure designed to reduce sexual performance anxiety. The steps on the hierarchy were:

1. Going into a situation where the possibility of meeting a woman exists
2. Going out with a woman for the first time
3. Petting with a woman with clothes on
4. Petting with a woman while naked
5. Having oral sex
6. Going out with a woman repeatedly, with the increased probability of intercourse
7. Having intercourse
8. Experiencing fast ejaculation
9. Attempting intercourse a second time, after an initial failure

Each week a new desensitization scene was added. The client was given the assignment of acting on each successive item in the hierarchy after he had imagined the scene with minimal anxiety. The following are examples of some of the desensitization scenes presented to Jim during hypnosis:

*Scene 4.* Now imagine going somewhere with Cindy (a woman recently met) where the possibility of intercourse exists. See yourself maintaining your state of calmness, removing any pressures to perform. Remove all those demands. Remind yourself that you do have the option to go only as far as you choose and that we have decided for this week you will not go beyond petting. That is what being assertive is: Your choosing to do something and also your choosing not to do something. And as you imagine this scene, rate how anxious you feel on that scale from 0–100 right now. (Client reports no anxiety.)

Now see yourself and Cindy petting. (pause) Both of you have your clothes off. You're both naked. You're touching her. How are you feeling as you imagine yourself caressing and touching her? What would you rate your anxiety level? (Client responds "20," which is minimal anxiety.)

Okay. Fine. Now, imagine her touching you. And now how are you feeling on that scale? (Client reports no anxiety.)

*Scene 5.* Imagine having oral sex with Cindy. You're lying back receiving oral sex. Now, how are you feeling on a scale from 0–100? (Client reports no anxiety.)

Just imagining receiving oral sex from Cindy, allowing yourself to just passively enjoy it. (pause)

*Scene 6.* Now imagine yourself going out with Cindy repeatedly, continuing to see her when you know it could lead to sexual intercourse. Recognizing the probability that, if you continue seeing her, it will eventually lead to intercourse. Now, as you consider these thoughts, what are you feeling on the scale from 0–100? (Client reports 60.)

Okay. You can bring down that tension. See what it is that is going through your mind right now that is generating the anxiety. Are you putting pressure on yourself to satisfy her? Pressure to perform? You can remove that pressure by just reminding yourself that you have the option to go at your own pace. And that you really will only have intercourse with her when it's the right time for you, no matter what she wants.

Now, as you remind yourself of that, even though you recognize the probability that eventually you will attempt intercourse with her, how are you feeling on that scale from 0–100? (Client reports 40.)

Good. You notice the effect of removing the pressure, giving yourself permission to do as you please at your pace. It has an immediate effect on reducing your anxiety. Now, you just continue relaxing away any tension.

And, again, think about continuing to see this woman, knowing it could lead to sexual intercourse. Really think about that. And now, how are you doing on a scale from 0–100? (Client reports 20.)

Good. Notice what your thoughts are about this. You are probably not demanding that you have to perform or live up to her expectations.

## Cognitive Restructuring

Cognitive restructuring for sexual difficulties involves the modification of sexually inhibiting thoughts so that the client views the sexual situation realistically and constructively. We assume that the removal of negative thinking will in turn reduce negative feelings that often interfere with sexual responsiveness.

One variation of cognitive restructuring, the two-column method, involves writing down thoughts that interfere with sexual feelings and behavior and replacing them with sexually enhancing thoughts. A married woman, Gloria (who sought hypnotherapy from W. G.), reported having experienced only one orgasm in her life. During that experience, she had noticed her rapid heart rate and breathing and become frightened that she was going to die. Since then, she had experienced desire and arousal but not orgasm (not even with the assistance of a vibrator). Through evocative imagery during hypnosis, she discovered the following negative thoughts about orgasm: "It's giving myself too much attention. I might lose control or die. I can't ask my husband for what I want; it's too selfish." Pre-orgasmic sensations engendered fear of dying or loss of control. When approaching pre-orgasmic sensations, she would tighten up and stop the stimulation.

With the two-column method, her negative thoughts were written down in one column, and a second column listed positive self-suggestions to replace the self-defeating ones (Table 7.2). Gloria's homework included self-hypnotic relaxation, followed by masturbation. She was asked to create a pleasant atmosphere with flowers and use of oils and to consider that she was making love to herself. First, she was able to induce orgasm by using a vibrator while imagining having intercourse with her husband. Then, during sexual encounters with her husband, she directed him to stimulate her manually and orally to orgasm. Although she never reached orgasm during intercourse, she and her husband were satisfied with her experiencing orgasm manually and orally. She was reassured by the therapist, who informed her that most women do not reach orgasm during intercourse.

Table 7.2. Sample Two-Column Method

| Negative Thoughts | Therapeutic Suggestions |
| --- | --- |
| 1. It's giving myself too much attention. | 1. I have a right to pleasure. |
| 2. I might lose control or die. | 2. It's safe. It's a healthy feeling. |
| 3. I can't ask my husband for what I want sexually. It's too selfish. | 3. It's okay to enjoy myself with my husband. I do want him to please me so I will ask him to do certain things (sexually). |

## Imaginal Rehearsal

The therapeutic technique of imaginal or mental rehearsal is intended to build confidence by having the client imagine success in sexual encounters where he or she has had difficulty. This imagery technique also provides the client with an opportunity to mentally rehearse specific techniques for improving sexual performance. For example, a fast ejaculator can be instructed to imagine himself pausing or slowing the pace of his thrusting as he approaches orgasm.

Imaginal rehearsal can be used in the treatment of any of the sexual dysfunctions and can be combined with erotic imagery. The only caution in using imaginal rehearsal is to be sure that the client does not experience it as a demand to perform. Performance pressures can be reduced by combining mental rehearsal with cognitive restructuring, as illustrated in the following case treated by F. F.:

Michael reported fast ejaculation, which left his partner unsatisfied and him with feelings of inadequacy. Evocative imagery revealed that he was impatient to have intercourse once sexual contact began. After intromission occurred, he ejaculated immediately. He felt completely helpless to control his orgasm. His negative thoughts regarding sexual encounters included I must have intercourse quickly, and What if I come too fast again? She'll be so disappointed again. What a failure I'll be.

To treat the problem, Michael initially learned and practiced hypnotic relaxation to reduce chronic anxiety. Furthermore, he was given this suggestion to reduce impatience: "Let me enjoy sexual feelings, rather than think I must have intercourse right away." And for thoughts of sexual failure and performance failure: "I will accept myself with the problem, rather than get upset about it. I can learn to control it." These positive self-suggestions were combined with mental rehearsal, during which Michael imagined himself using breathing techniques and other methods to exert greater control over ejaculation.

The following self-hypnotic script containing mental rehearsal and relaxation suggestions was developed for Michael:

> I am focusing on my breathing. Easy breathing; there is no rush. Saying "re. . . . .lax" with every breath; enjoy feelings of sexual arousal, yet remaining calm, not frenzied. As I think about regaining control slowly, one step at a time, I feel more confident, less overwhelmed. Now slowly beginning to enter her . . . focusing on my breathing, pacing myself . . . a slow, deliberate stroking with my penis. Taking control . . . possibly feeling pre-orgasmic sensations . . . slowing down even more, to regain control, re-focusing on saying "re. . . . .lax" with each breath. Delaying orgasm for even a few seconds more than before . . . every second is more control.

After mentally rehearsing ejaculatory control for 2 weeks, he was able to apply these techniques during sexual encounters with his partner, first during manual and oral sex and eventually during intercourse. Michael learned to control his orgasmic response and was able to prolong intercourse.

## Hypno-assertion

Improvement of sexual responsiveness could require direct requests to a partner for specific types of sexual caressing or stimulation. The client can develop effective self-expression using hypno-assertion, which involves visualizing the performance of assertive behaviors. Such imaginal assertion can be combined with hypnotic desensitization to reinforce stepwise progression from imaginal to *in vivo* assertion.

Sue's longtime male friend regularly proceeded to sexual intercourse with almost no foreplay. Sue felt dominated by him and feared that asserting her own needs, including sexual needs, would anger him and possibly cause him to end the relationship. Therefore, she settled for an unsatisfactory sexual relationship. The following suggestions were developed by Sue and her therapist (F. F.) to alleviate her anxieties about rejection and assert herself in the sexual situation:

> You want to feel good about sex with Bob, not just be used. And you can feel good about it by telling him that you want more touching and holding before intercourse. That is important to you. You know he probably won't leave just because you speak up, and, if he did just because you expressed yourself, it isn't worth stifling yourself in order to keep the relationship. Now, see yourself asking for what you want. It feels good. You will do it, feeling stronger, more confident. You will do it!

Sue was instructed during hypnosis to imagine herself being assertive during sexual encounters with her friend:

> Imagine yourself gently suggesting to your partner that he stimulate you in a way that you desire. You also suggest that he slow down foreplay, to proceed at your pace. You focus on your feelings of pleasure, rather than just his. You take responsibility for your feelings and understand that his discomforts or reactions to your new assertiveness are not your fault. His discomforts belong to him. You are sharing with him, rather than hurting him. Better sexual communication is the goal. Yes, feeling better about your new assertiveness.

Using self-hypnosis with these suggestions, she was able to convince herself to make sexual requests. Her friend was supportive and did make efforts to prolong foreplay.

## Hypnotic Aversion Therapy

In the 1960s and the early 1970s, a body of behavior therapy literature emerged that addressed modification of homosexual behavior, pedophilia, voyeurism, exhibitionism, fetishism, and a number of less common sexual preferences. Aversion therapy, the most commonly reported intervention, involved pairing shock or nausea, evoked through drugs or hypnosis, with sexual fantasies or pictures illustrating the client's unwanted sexual preferences.

Cautela (1967) coined the term *covert sensitization*, an aversion therapy procedure that employs imagery to create both sexual and aversive stimuli. The unpleasant mental image used as an aversive stimulus involves description of the client becoming nauseous and vomiting when attempting to engage in the undesirable sexual behavior. Usually an *aversion-relief* paradigm is employed, whereby the suggestions of nausea are terminated as the client is asked to imagine stopping himself or herself from performing the sexual behavior he or she wishes to eliminate.

Aversive imagery can also include realistic negative consequences of the unwanted sexual behavior. For example, homosexuals wanting to change their behavior so that they no longer engage in unsafe sex can be asked to imagine themselves getting AIDS. Also, pedophiles and exhibitionists can be asked to imagine themselves getting caught. Many of these individuals are impulsive and either do not consider or reject possible negative consequences. An example of how hypnosis can be applied to problematic sexual preferences is illustrated by the case of Harry.

Harry, an unmarried traveling salesman, sought treatment from W. G. for exhibitionism. The client would go out and stalk young, attractive women in their teens or twenties. He would then expose himself in front of selected women in a public place. The exhibitionism was triggered either by feelings of sexual desire or negative feelings of anxiety, anger, depression, or inadequacy, especially if he had been recently rejected or felt lonely. His flashing was a method of striking back at women for having been rejected and for feeling lonely, and it also served to reduce anxiety and distract himself from upset feelings, such as worries about his job.

The basic therapeutic strategy was twofold. *First*, suppress Harry's exhibitionism through hypnotic aversion therapy and redirect his feelings toward appropriate sexual choices. *Second*, help him control feelings of anxiety, anger, and depression, so that they would no longer serve as triggers for exhibitionism.

Initially, hypnotic aversion (a combination of covert sensitization and hypnosis) was introduced. While hypnotized, Harry imagined a woman he would find attractive. It was suggested that he visualize a situation where he could exhibit himself in front of her. Then the hypnotic script suggested the following aversive feelings:

> Now, visualizing the situation. You are looking at the attractive woman. You think about flashing, thinking about it more and more. . . . Now, you start to get a sick feeling in the pit of your stomach; yes, a sick feeling in your gut. It's welling up inside of you; more intense, your eyes are getting teary. The unbearable feeling of retching is overcoming you. Now, you are aware of food coming up your throat, the sickening, disgusting feeling of food coming up your throat, being expelled from your mouth. You're vomiting all over yourself, all over your clothes. It smells horrible.
>
> But it stops now. It stops as soon as you say to yourself, "I'm not going to flash. No, I'm not going to flash." You say this over and over. And you feel an enormous sense of relief . . . such wonderful relief. Your breathing is becoming slow and deep. It feels so good breathing clean fresh air . . . such pleasant feelings all over.

In addition, hypnotic aversion focused on the punishing image that he *would get caught by the police*. The client participated in creating this scene by thinking of 10 different ways he could get caught for each situation in which he would typically flash. Thus, the hypnotic aversion treatment had both a conditioning component, the aversive stimulus itself, and a problem-solving component, teaching realistic consequences of his actions. Then the client was taught self-hypnosis and instructed to re-create the effects of the hypnotic aversion treatment during home practice and *in vivo*, whenever he felt the impulse to flash.

In the second phase of treatment, hypnosis was used to reduce his anxiety. He was taught self-hypnotic relaxation to control anxiety that had previously led to exhibitionism. Also, suggestions such as "Just because I get rejected doesn't mean I'm worthless" were incorporated into the client's self-hypnosis to further reduce feelings of depression, anger, and inadequacy. Instead of acting out his negative feelings through flashing, the client was encouraged to think of alternatives (problem solving) such as calling friends when he felt lonely. Private masturbation was prescribed as a sexual alternative to reduce arousal levels that could have contributed to exhibitionism.

Finally, as the exhibitionism was reduced, the therapist taught the client a variety of appropriate social skills so that he might find a girlfriend, which he eventually did.

## SUMMARY

Hypnosis can be a powerful tool in the treatment of sexual problems, even when a cooperative sexual partner is unavailable. Preliminary empirical support for treating sexual problems through hypnosis has been reported by Araoz (1982, 1984). On the basis of clinical data, he found hypnotic treatment of sexual dysfunction to be more effective than traditional sex therapy. Replication of these positive results awaits further research.

# Chapter 8

# Overcoming Resistance In Hypnotherapy

According to the traditional psychoanalytic position, resistance is inevitable because it is inherent in the defenses the client uses to ward off anxiety and guilt. Because resistance occurs as a defense against the elicitation of frightening unconscious material, its presence is to be expected in therapeutic approaches that concentrate on providing clients with insight into unconscious conflicts.

Erickson and strategic therapists such as Haley (1976) recognized that resistance is always a possibility in therapy, even when hypnosis is used. Rossi (Erickson et al. 1976) stated "we invariably doubt and test any suggestion that is made to us" (p. 216). However, instead of attempting to overcome resistance through interpretation and insight, Erickson and his followers have attempted to bypass or overcome resistance through indirect methods such as utilizing the client's resistance, paradoxical interventions, therapeutic binds, indirect suggestions, and confusion techniques, which will be discussed later in the chapter.

Only recently have cognitive–behavioral therapists begun to recognize and examine resistance. Originally Wolpe and Lazarus (1968) claimed that resistance did not exist in behavior therapy. More recently, Lazarus and Fay (1982) argued that the concept of resistance is a rationalization used by therapists to explain away their failures. Wolpe and Lazarus and Lazarus and Fay objected to the concept of resistance because they felt it implied that the client was at fault and it allowed the therapist to avoid taking responsibility for the outcome of therapy. On the other hand, Lazarus and Fay's proposal that all treatment failures are either the fault of the therapist or the therapeutic method goes to the opposite extreme and frees the client of any responsibility for treatment outcome.

Operating from a social psychology perspective, Brehm (1966) has developed the concept of *psychological reactance* to account for one type of resistance. Reactance is defined as a motivational state referring to an individual's tendency to resist perceived or actual threats to his or her freedom. Reactance, in part, accounts for the "oppositional client" familiar to every therapist. Although Brehm originally thought of reactance as caused by specific situations only, Dowd and Milne (1986), among others, have argued that there are individual differences in reactance that account for the different degrees of oppositional behavior in clients. Using these ideas, Dowd, Milne, and Wise (1984) have developed a paper-and-pencil measure of psychological reactance, The Therapeutic Reactance Scale. By using this measure, therapists can tailor their treatment to the type of client involved by determining in advance the level of potential reactance. A copy of the scale and the scoring instructions are included in the appendix.

## SOURCES OF RESISTANCE

Rather than blaming either therapists or clients for treatment failures, a more objective approach would be to examine all of the possible factors that could account for a client's resistance to treatment. Once a particular source of resistance is identified, then a decision can be made about how and when to intervene. Golden (1983b) has listed 3 sources of resistance.

### Therapy and therapist factors

1. Absence of rapport between therapist and client
2. Failure to identify the relevant antecedent, or maintaining variables, or both
3. Failure to see that the client is avoiding a higher order anxiety (for example, an overweight client fearing that, if she lost weight, she would have to deal with her social and sexual anxieties about dating men)
4. Incorrect use of proper technique (usually because of lack of experience or training)
5. Initiation of treatment although the client does not understand or accept the rationale for it
6. Incorrect or irrelevant homework assignment or intervention with regard to the client's goals
7. Too threatening or anxiety-provoking an assignment or step in the therapeutic procedure
8. Too time-consuming an assignment
9. Inadequacies in the available treatment techniques and approaches for dealing with a particular problem

## Environmental and other external factors

1. Deliberate sabotage from others (for example, threats of rejection or disapproval for being more assertive or successful)
2. Inadvertent sabotage from others such as family members who become "benevolent saboteurs" for example, the individual who inadvertently reinforces a family member's agoraphobia by chauffering the phobic person around, thus providing him or her with secondary gain for being phobic
3. Other secondary gains such as those from disability and welfare benefits, which provide clients with reinforcement for their "disabilities"

## Client factors

1. Cognitions, such as self-fulfilling prophecies and negative expectations (for example, the belief that "I'll never succeed so why try"), low frustration tolerance (the tendency to avoid all discomfort), and demands that lead to self-defeating maneuvers (for example, the insomniac who insists that he or she must get to sleep and tries to force sleep)
2. "Hidden agendas" or nonverbalized issues that could interfere with treatment (for example, the individual who has no intention of working on a relationship but who pushes his or her spouse into marital therapy, with the secret intention of leaving the marriage)
3. Motivation (that is, when a client does not value the desired outcome of therapy enough to devote the necessary time and effort to change)
4. High level of psychological reactance and resulting need for countercontrol
5. Neurological and other biological limitations

# STRATEGIES FOR PREVENTING RESISTANCE

Research on compliance from the areas of social psychology, cognitive-behavior therapy and behavioral medicine has resulted in several recommendations that we have found to be useful in preventing resistance in hypnotherapy:

1. Educate the client concerning the treatment and its rationale. The same advice is offered by Meichenbaum and Gilmore (1982) with regard to reducing resistance in cognitive–behavioral therapy. They point out that having a shared conceptualization with the client about his or her problem is very important because cognitive–behavioral interventions follow directly from the conceptualization of the client's problem. If the client does not accept or understand the treatment rationale, he or she is unlikely to comply

with it. In Ericksonian therapy it is less likely that the treatment methods will seem logically related to the client's problems. Nevertheless, Haley (1976) has mentioned the importance of providing the client with a rationale for even paradoxical techniques (discussed later in the chapter) such as prescribing the symptom and encouraging a relapse. One possible explanation that can be offered to the client for these interventions is that much can be learned about one's problem by having a relapse or by purposely engaging in symptomatic behavior. The *law of reverse effect* is another possible explanation that can be offered to explain paradoxical instructions. Clients suffering from symptoms such as insomnia, blushing, and excessive sweating can be told that, the harder one tries to control functions that are under the control of the autonomic nervous system, the more one fails. Therefore, trying to intensify one's symptom will break the vicious cycle and reduce the symptom. As Haley (1976) pointed out, it is not necessary for the rationale to be correct. It only needs to be convincing and believable.

2. Tailor the treatment so that it fits into the client's daily routine. In other words, program the therapeutic requirements within a realistic schedule. Make sure the assignment is not too time consuming. In relating this recommendation to hypnosis, the authors have found that a client is more likely to practice self-hypnosis if the exercises are tailored to his or her preferences. For example, some clients protest that they are too restless or too busy to practice self-hypnosis for the length of time suggested by their therapists. But, when the exercises are shortened to the length preferred by the clients, many of them do then cooperate.

3. Use "shaping" or successive approximations with clients receiving complex treatments. Instead of asking a client to adhere to a complex treatment right away, it is better to introduce elements of the program one at a time and wait for the client to respond to each element before introducing additional parts or techniques. An example of this tactic is Erickson's treatment of a compulsive washer. The first intervention was merely to instruct the client to change his brand of soap. Erickson then had the client use different towels, then take showers at different times, and so on. A similar approach is used in systematic desensitization. The idea is to break down an anxiety or phobia into smaller, more manageable steps and have the client confront the easiest first.

4. Make use of self-monitoring techniques. Having clients monitor and keep records of their therapeutic activities increases the likelihood that they will adhere to the program.

Self-monitoring procedures have been routinely used by cognitive and behavior therapists. Although hypnotherapists tend to be less empirical in monitoring the progress of their clients, self-monitoring is quite compatible with hypnotherapy. However, it seems that many of the clients seeking hypnosis are looking for a magical cure that will not involve effort on their part. These clients are typically resistant to keeping records. One gambit employed by the authors is to make hypnosis contingent upon satisfactory completion of self-monitoring assignments. This contingency-management procedure forces passive clients to take a more active role. We have found that the contingency is effective in getting passive clients to self-monitor so long as the therapist is consistent and refuses to proceed with hypnosis until the client brings in data. We have found that few clients quit and seek out another hypnotist, so long as the resistance is addressed. Most clients simply do the self-monitoring in order to get the hypnosis.

Another advantage of including self-monitoring procedures at the beginning of the therapy is that they are reactive, that is, clients often experience improvement as a result of the self-monitoring alone. It shows clients prior to hypnosis that change can occur. Many of them are rather surprised at this discovery. They often report feeling encouraged by these results, and they are more hopeful and seem to have more confidence in the therapy.

5. Whenever possible, make use of social support from family and friends to encourage the client and reinforce him or her for adhering to the treatment program. Although interpersonal factors are often neglected in hypnotherapy, they can be valuable in overcoming resistance. Family members can be enlisted as therapy aids in the treatment programs, such as in exposure therapy for phobias. After hypnotic desensitization, the client still needs to confront his or her fears in reality. Even when hypnosis is used to reduce anxiety, most clients still report feeling anxious during *in vivo* exposure. Support and encouragement from family can sometimes make the difference in whether the client follows through or not. Also, smaller, more manageable steps are made possible by having family members accompany the client into the feared situations before the client goes into them alone. In addition, enlisting family members early can help prevent them from sabotaging therapeutic progress later.

6. Involve the client in the selection of techniques and the construction of assignments. Many therapists have emphasized that resistance is reduced when the client is provided with choices.

As we pointed out in chapter 2, the client can be involved in the decision about which hypnotic induction procedure will be used. The various methods can be described, and the client can state a preference. Also, instead of standardized images being used, the client can be asked to construct his or her own. After being taught how to formulate suggestions, the client can also be involved in constructing the hypnotic suggestions the therapist uses in treatment. The development of self-hypnotic skills is also facilitated in this manner.

Erickson also recognized the importance of allowing the client to make choices in his or her response to hypnotic suggestion. His general approach was to be permissive in letting the client respond to suggestions in his or her own unique ways. As Erickson and others have pointed out, ambiguity, generalization, and open-ended suggestions elicit the client's own unique associations, predispositions, and potentialities. The following are some examples of open-ended suggestions:

"You may be aware of a certain sensation."

"We all have potentials we are unaware of, and we usually don't know how they will be expressed."

"This week you might begin to notice some change taking place."

Open-ended suggestions like those just described allow the client a great deal of freedom in how he or she responds. Even when Erickson wanted to focus the client's response in a particular direction, he formulated his suggestions so that they would provide the client with several alternatives. See chapter 2 for more information on how to employ Erickson's techniques for hypnotic induction.

7. Capitalize on the expectations and requests of the client. Resistance is reduced when the therapist matches the treatment method to the client's expectations and requests. Most clients do much better if they are given what they want. Thus, most clients who come in for hypnotherapy should be provided with it.

8. Anticipate difficulties and setbacks and prepare the client for them. In Marlatt and Gordon's (1980) cognitive–behavioral relapse-prevention program, the therapist and the client identify high-risk situations and thoughts that could lead to relapse. The client is taught to anticipate these "triggers" in advance and to plan coping strategies for dealing with them. A similar technique is used by Ericksonian therapists (Haley, 1976). The therapist predicts a relapse or instructs the client to have one. Either the client has the relapse as predicted or the client continues to improve. Either way the therapist's credibility is maintained. This method is particularly helpful when a client has shown some initial improvement. At this point, the client can become overly enthusiastic and unrealistic about future progress. Unless the therapist prepares him or her for the plateaus and regressions that naturally take place during the course of treatment, he or she can easily become discouraged. Predicting setbacks actually provides the client with more realistic expectations about progress in therapy.

A similar technique involves anticipating or preempting resistance (Watzlawick, 1978) and is especially useful with oppositional clients. When it is suspected that a client will be resistant, the therapist can defuse the resistance by predicting it before it occurs. Before assigning a therapeutic task, the therapist expresses some reservations about it such as "I think this would really help but you're probably not ready to do it yet," or "you're probably going to think this is too hard for you to do *right now*." The effect of these preempting statements is twofold; the client either opposes the therapist and does the assignment, or the credibility of the therapist is maintained even though the client does not accept the assignment.

9. Use a variety of methods for distracting the client, so that he or she doesn't have the opportunity to build up resistance. Research in social psychology has shown that distraction from a message can reduce later resistance to that message (see Festinger & Maccoby, 1964).

There are several ways of distracting a client. One is by using multiple tasks. Erickson would often assign absorbing tasks such as listening to music, while, at the same time, he would make other suggestions. One can also ask the client to count backward from 999 to 1 by threes. According to Erickson, methods such as these "depotentiate" or bypass consciousness and reduce the likelihood of resistance. Erickson believed that the unconscious becomes more receptive to suggestion when the conscious mind is confused or distracted by an absorbing task (Erickson & Rossi, 1979).

Another hypnotic induction procedure involving multiple tasks is the eye-fixation method. It usually begins with asking the client to look at a spot and notice whatever sensations develop in the eyelids. This method appears to be more powerful when the hypnotist does not continue to focus on eye fixation and closure but instead assigns eye fixation to the client, while the hypnotist talks about other things such as relaxation or breathing. The following induction procedure, which the reader can find in greater detail in chapter 2, illustrates the eye-fixation method involving multiple tasks and alternative ways of responding:

'You can pick a spot, any will do, and keep on staring at it. If your eyes should wander, just go back to the same spot. Just keep on staring at it until your eyes become tired of it; then you can close your eyes and enter a pleasant, relaxed state. While you stare at that spot, you might notice some interesting phenomena. Some people experience a blurring of their vision, whereas for others, the spot moves, pulsates, or disappears. The really important thing is for you to notice whatever it is that you experience and to enjoy it. And while you continue to focus on that spot, you can let yourself sink into the chair and begin to relax. . . .

Another way of distracting the client is by using the interspersal method, or embedded suggestions. In this method, certain suggestions are embedded within the content of a story that seems to have little to do with the client's problem. The embedded suggestions are usually vocally stressed.

An example of Erickson's interspersal technique with embedded suggestions is his treatment of Joe, a florist, who was in pain from cancer. Although Joe was resistant to hypnosis, his family asked Erickson to treat him. Erickson did not even discuss hypnosis with Joe, but, in response to Joe's question about what Erickson wanted, Erickson immediately launched into what appeared to be casual conversation about gardening and tomato plants. However, Erickson interspersed hypnotic suggestions in between his comments about the tomato plant. The following is a small segment of the induction procedure (embedded suggestions are capitalized by the present authors):

> . . . Now, as I talk, and I can do so COMFORTABLY, I wish that you would LISTEN TO ME COMFORTABLY, as I talk about a tomato plant. That is an odd thing to talk about. It makes one CURIOUS. WHY TALK ABOUT A TOMATO PLANT? One puts a tomato seed in the ground. One can FEEL HOPE that it WILL GROW into a tomato plant that WILL BRING SATISFACTION by the fruit it has. The seed soaks up water, not very much difficulty in doing that because of the rains that BRING PEACE AND COMFORT and the joy of growing to flowers and tomatoes. . . . (Haley, 1973, p. 262).

Another way of distracting clients is by using a confusion routine. This is a discussion that constantly shifts focus and direction but has a central underlying message. Because it is almost impossible for the client to logically follow the discussion, it becomes easier not to try. Because the higher level mental processes of censoring and evaluating are temporarily at rest, the client can hear the central message with less resistance. Construction of confusion routines is not an easy task (it is easy for the therapist to also become confused, and we recommend that examples in the writings of Erickson be studied (for example, Erickson, Rossi & Rossi, 1976, Erickson & Rossi, 1979).

10. Use the *foot-in-the-door* technique. Erickson frequently made use of the foot-in-the-door concept and would develop what he called a *yes set* for cooperative behavior (Erickson, et al. 1976). The basic strategy is to make small requests or ask the client to accomplish very small tasks before asking for more. The foot-in-the-door approach is used to reduce resistance by establishing a cooperative set that predisposes the individual to continue cooperating.

In therapy there are many ways in which the foot-in-the-door approach can be applied. Simply asking the client to do very small things such as sit in another chair can be an initial step in establishing a yes set. In hypnosis the use of pacing and leading can establish a yes set. As noted before, in pacing, the therapist feeds back to the client behaviors that the therapist observes the client already doing, or he or she describes experiences in such an open-ended manner that the client responds with his or her own associations. All of these methods help create a cooperative mode in the client. Basically, the idea is to get the client to cooperate in very small ways or to merely lead him or her to believe he or she is cooperating no matter what he or she is doing.

## STRATEGIES FOR OVERCOMING RESISTANCE

There are two ways of handling resistance when it occurs, direct and indirect.

## Direct Methods

One of the authors has outlined a problem-solving approach that can be used to overcome resistance (Golden, 1983b). It involves a reassesment of therapy whenever resistance is encountered. The therapist and the client work together on the impasse as a problem to be solved. The client is taught to employ the same methods used in therapy to deal with any problem: self-monitoring, cognitive restructuring, training in the development of new skills needed to overcome the problem, desensitization to higher order anxieties, and so on. Here is an outline of the program for dealing with resistance recommended by Golden (1983b):

1. Note the resistance and invite the client to explore the reason for it.
2. Examine possible therapist factors.
3. Reevaluate the goals of the client and his or her understanding of the treatment. Evaluate whether the treatment and assignments are relevant to the client's goals.
4. Negotiate smaller changes in behavior if the recommended ones are too anxiety provoking.
5. Consider environmental and interpersonal factors that maintain the problem. Join the client against people purposely trying to sabotage his or her changing. Turn benevolent saboteurs into allies. For example, educate family members about treatment and include them in it as therapy assistants.
6. Help the client identify any thoughts, feelings, behaviors, reinforcing consequences, and higher order anxieties that are interfering with change.
7. Reconceptualize and work on higher order anxieties. For example, an agoraphobic client stopped following through on her *in vivo* assignments after some initial progress. An examination of the resistance revealed her fear of having to face the responsibilities of work and marriage once she overcame her agoraphobia. The focus of therapy then shifted to helping her overcome these fears before returning to the treatment of agoraphobia.
8. Look for "hidden agendas" and secondary gains. Explore and evaluate, with the client, the consequences and the pros and cons of changing. Look for additional payoffs and benefits of changing versus not changing, which the client might not have realized or considered. Explore, with the client, in what way life would be better or worse if change were to occur.
9. Use cognitive restructuring to modify maladaptive emotions such as anxiety, guilt, embarrassment, or low frustration tolerance that are interfering with the client's ability to comply with therapeutic instructions and assignments.
10. Employ rewards and penalties to encourage compliance with difficult clients.

11. Consider indirect methods such as those from Ericksonian therapy when all else fails (for example, joining the resistance)

An example of the problem-solving approach for dealing with resistance in hypnotherapy is the case of Barbara. As a result of the therapist (W. G.) and the client's exploring the possible reasons why Barbara was not responding to hypnotic desensitization, she disclosed that she was not practicing or applying self-hypnosis. Her resistance was due to her belief that she was incapable of using self-hypnosis and was depending on the therapist to cure her. The focus of therapy shifted toward helping Barbara with her feelings of helplessness and inadequacy. These feelings caused her to take an overly dependent role in therapy. Various techniques such as cognitive restructuring, risk taking, and successive approximations (shaping) were used to overcome Barbara's helplessness to the point where she was able to successfully apply self-hypnosis in the reduction of her fears. See chapter 9 on self-hypnosis training for more details of the case.

## Indirect Methods

Although the direct problem-solving approach to overcoming resistance is often successful, there are clients for whom it is not appropriate. Clients who will not cooperate (oppositional clients) and those whose symptoms become worse when they try to cooperate might benefit from a more indirect approach. Two strategies in particular that have been found to be helpful are paradoxical interventions and Erickson's utilization techniques.

## Paradoxical Interventions

Paradoxical instructions can be given during hypnosis but are also effective alone. Dowd and Milne (1986) have described several types of paradoxical interventions. In *symptom prescription*, the client is instructed to engage in the actual problem behavior or even to exaggerate it; for example, the insomniac is told to deliberately try staying awake, instead of trying to sleep. In using *restraining*, the therapist either discourages the client from changing at all or changing too quickly or predicts a relapse. In *positioning* the therapist joins the resistance and agrees with the client's negative statements.

Some caution is required in using paradoxical interventions. As Dowd and Milne pointed out, sometimes the use of paradoxical interventions is neither wise nor ethical. They, and we, strongly advise the reader to avoid using paradoxical instructions that, if carried out by a client, would lead to negative consequences such as violence, suicide, homicide, excessive drinking, drug abuse, illegal actions, or behavior that could be harmful to self or others. Paradox is also not recommended with disorganized and mentally retarded individuals and in crisis situations such as in acute grief reactions. Caution should also be taken in using paradox with sociopaths, paranoids, clients with borderline personalities, and very depressed clients.

Dowd and Milne (1986) have also discussed the types of paradoxical interventions appropriate for low- and high-reactant clients. Low-reactant clients are cooperative, whereas high-reactant clients are oppositional and defiant. Reactance level can be assessed by interview behavior, such as constant disagreement with the therapist, or by consistent noncompletion of homework assignments, or by a paper-and-pencil measure such as the Therapeutic Reactance Scale (Dowd et al., 1984) discussed at the beginning of the chapter.

Defiance-based strategies are useful for high-reactant clients and are based on the assumption that the client will defy the directive and thereby improve. An example is the restraining technique of inhibiting change, in which the therapist encourages the client not to overcome the problem too quickly. A high-reactant client defies this directive and changes more quickly. It is important not to let defiant clients know the real intent of the paradoxical instructions, or they might act in a contrary fashion. Positioning is also useful as a defiance-based strategy with high-reactant clients. For example, agreeing with high-reactant clients that they cannot change often results in change. It is important to only use defiance-based strategies with high-reactant clients. Telling low-reactant clients that they cannot change does not produce change, only demoralization.

Compliance-based strategies are useful for low-reactant clients and are based on the assumption that the client will improve by carrying out the directive. Certain types of paradoxical interventions are appropriate for low-reactant clients. As Watzlawik, Weakland, and Fisch (1974) pointed out, many times the solutions clients use in attempting to solve their problems make things worse rather than improving the situation. There are a number of conditions (for example, insomnia, blushing, excessive sweating, erectile dysfunction, premature and retarded ejaculation, and orgasmic dysfunction) where attempts to use 'will power" or to try harder usually increase anxiety and make things worse. Symptom prescription is useful for low-reactant clients with these conditions, because the very attempt to comply with the paradoxical directive interferes with the clients' ineffective strategy of trying too hard. An example is the insomniac who has previously tried to fall asleep, only to make the problem worse. Instructions (which can be given during hypnosis but are also effective without hypnosis) to try to remain awake as long as possible are effective with cooperative (low-reactant) clients because they attempt to follow the directive. In attempting to comply with these instructions, clients stop trying to fall asleep and sleep more easily.

## Utilization Techniques

The application of utilization strategies is most obviously illustrated by the work of Milton Erickson. Whenever Erickson was confronted with resistance, he attempted to utilize it in a therapeutic way instead of confronting it or opposing it. Erickson has used an excellent analogy to describe his utilization of resistance: "a person who wants to change the course of a river. If he opposes the river by trying to block it, the river will merely go over and around him. But if he accepts the force of the river and diverts it in a new direction the force of the river will cut a new channel" (in Haley, 1973, p. 8). Another useful analogy has been offered by Watzlawick (1978), who described the approach as psychological judo. Instead of getting into a power struggle with a client and exerting greater force against the resistance, it is better to yield to it and use the client's resistance in a positive way.

An example of the utilization of resistance is Erickson's treatment of a 12-year-old, 170-lb boy who was described by his parents as a rebellious, stubborn, uncooperative, chronic bed wetter. When Erickson invited the boy into his office, he resisted and said "he was tired enough to go to sleep and that he would rather go home." Erickson responded by acknowledging that the boy could defeat him "by deliberately going to sleep and not listening." Erickson reported that the boy accepted the "challenge," and trance was induced through suggestions such as "Just go to sleep, just don't listen to me; you can sleep restfully and comfortably, even if I do talk . . ." (Erickson, 1952, pp. 229–230). Erickson then proceeded to give suggestions such as the following:

> Your parents want you to have a permanently dry bed right away, and that is simply unreasonable. In the first place you have been too busy to learn to have a dry bed. . . . But you will soon be full grown, bigger than your father, and you haven't got far to go to beat him. Then you'll have all that energy and horse power you have been putting into growing to spread around to the other things you want, like a permanently dry bed. In fact, you are so close to being finished with building that great big powerful body that you've probably already got extra energy to spare.

> But let's get it straight. I don't think its reasonable to expect you to have a permanently dry bed this month—it's only the first part of January. I don't even expect you to have just one dry bed this week. That's too darned soon. It's not reasonable. But what puzzles me is whether you will have a dry bed next week on Wednesday or on Thursday. I don't know and you don't know and we'll have to wait to find out, and that is a long wait because today is only Monday of this week and you really won't know until Friday of next week whether you will have a dry bed on Wednesday or Thursday of next week . . . you can come in next Friday and let me know whether it was Wednesday or Thursday, and you will just have to wait and see (1952, pp. 230–231).

At the next session, the client reported that he had had a dry bed on both

Wednesday and Thursday. Erickson then proceeded to give similar suggestions for a permanent cessation of the boy's enuresis.

In this example, Erickson joined the resistance and utilized it as part of his hypnotic induction procedure with the boy. Then he used a series of *therapeutic binds*, which, as Watzlawick (1978) pointed out, provides clients with an "illusion of alternatives" (p. 108). It seems as though the client has alternative ways of responding to a therapeutic bind. However, if the bind is effective, then, no matter how the client responds, she or he gets better. Erickson created a therapeutic bind by stating that he did not expect the boy to have "just one dry bed" that week but was puzzled over whether it would be next Wednesday or next Thursday. The boy was put in a bind because he was given the choice of having a dry bed either on Wednesday or Thursday of the next week. Even if he wet the bed that week, he would still be complying with Erickson's suggestion. As mentioned above, the boy had a dry bed on both Wednesday and Thursday.

Another type of indirect suggestion used by Erickson in this case is *implication*. One example of implication is Erickson's statement "I don't think it's reasonable to expect you to have a permanently dry bed this month." Here, he indirectly suggested that the boy would have a dry night that month and that he would eventually undergo a permanent change. According to Erickson, indirect suggestions such as these are preferred because, under these conditions, the client is not fully aware of the relation between the suggestion and his or her response to it. When a client is unaware of the process, there is less opportunity for resistance.

## TREATING THE RESISTANT
## CLIENT: CASE EXAMPLES

### Case I

John was a community college student who sought treatment for test anxiety, poor concentration, and difficulty with studying. His functioning was minimal, and he did not have any friends. He worked as an unskilled laborer at night and had a long history of being a marginal student.

John insisted on hypnotic treatment but claimed he could not be hypnotized. He reported that he had been to five different hypnotists, who were all unable to hypnotize him. However, all used traditional hypnotic induction procedures that involved direct attempts to induce hypnosis.

The therapist (W. G.) felt that he was being set up to fail, just like the other therapists who had attempted to treat John through hypnosis as he had requested. On the one hand, John was demanding to be hypnotized. On the other hand, he was saying that he could not be hypnotized. The following *indirect-modeling induction* procedure was used immediately in response to John's challenge (Golden, 1986b, pp. 14–16):

> "You know you're right John, I can't hypnotize you, but I'll tell you what, I'll show you how I hypnotize myself."
>
> Without further ado, the therapist proceeded to demonstrate and teach John how he hypnotizes himself.
>
> "First, I find a comfortable position in a chair like this one or like the one you're sitting on. I let myself sink into the chair into a comfortable position." (The therapist paused and looked in John's direction. Apparently in response to the therapist's implicit suggestion, John repositioned himself in the chair. The therapist waited for John to get comfortable, before he went on.)
>
> "Usually I close my eyes, but I don't have to. But it often helps to close your eyes when *you* are first learning to relax." (The therapist was giving John indirect suggestions to relax. John was also being given choices, such as the choice to close his eyes or to keep them open and the choice to either experience relaxation or to simply listen and learn how one may go about hypnotizing himself.)
>
> The therapist closed his eyes for a few moments and continued to talk about how he hypnotizes himself. When the therapist opened his eyes again he saw the client was resting comfortably with his eyes closed.
>
> "Next, I take several long slow deep breaths . . . and each time I exhale, I start to let go of a little tension . . . letting my arms . . . and my legs go loose and limp . . . letting my body sink into the chair . . . letting my back go loose and limp . . . letting my shoulders hang comfortably . . . letting my jaws hang slack." (The therapist continued to model the breathing and progressive relaxation, occasionally opening his eyes, in order to observe John and pace his comments to match changes in the client's breathing, posture, and musculature.)
>
> As the client exhaled, the therapist suggested "and as you exhale you can sink further into the chair and experience a more relaxed feeling." (At this point the therapist switched from speaking about his own experiences, stopped using the word "I," and began leading by talking more directly to the client using the word "You.")
>
> After John exhibited signs of deep relaxation, he was given suggestions that now that he was relaxed, he could enter a deep hypnotic trance. Relaxation imagery, counting, and the image of walking down a long stairway were used as deepening techniques. Then before the trance was terminated, John was given suggestions that he was a good hypnotic subject and that he would be able to recreate the trance by repeating the procedure using the same techniques of deep breathing, progressive relaxation, imagining pleasant scenes, counting, and the stairway image. He was also given suggestions that during trance he would be receptive to constructive suggestions that would aid him in achieving his goals. It was then suggested that after he opened his eyes he could reinduce the trance because he now knew how to hypnotize himself. John responded to these suggestions, demonstrating that he could induce self-hypnosis, and at his next session, reported that he was practicing his self-hypnosis exercises several times a day.
>
> In subsequent sessions, John was cooperative and receptive to more direct methods. Imagery was used to identify self-defeating thoughts, attitudes, and fantasies. While in a trance, John was instructed to imagine himself in test-taking situations. Through this evocative technique John was able to identify

and report that he believed he was "stupid" and "worthless" and that he would fail no matter how much he studied. Also evoked by the imagery were a series of images or fantasies, in which John pictured himself going blank on tests and failing.

The treatment consisted of cognitive restructuring procedures that were utilized while the client was in trance. Imaginal rehearsal was the main technique used. The therapist gave John the following suggestions during hypnosis while John imagined himself in situations involving examinations:

"You can do well on your exam as long as you study. But no matter how you do, you are still worthwhile, and can treat yourself well." John was asked to imagine himself coping with the examination situation and responding appropriately by calming down and doing well on the exam.

A similar procedure was used for studying. After undergoing a hypnotic induction procedure John was taught study skills. He was asked to imagine himself using techniques such as mentally rehearsing important facts, distributing his study time, sticking to a schedule, taking notes, etc. He was also given suggestions about studying and for improved concentration such as the following:

"You are learning very well how to concentrate. Your ability to enter hypnosis is proof of this. And because you are becoming more relaxed about exams, you will be able to retrieve more information. . . . And you are learning more because you are learning how to study. And you are beginning to realize that no one can remember everything they read. You can do well even if you forget some important information."

After five hypnosis sessions, John reported feeling less anxious while studying and during examinations. He passed all of his exams and attained a 2.2 average, as compared with his past grade point average of 1.7. John continued to maintain these gains at follow-up one term later.

## Case II

Paul D. sought treatment for panic attacks. At first he requested behavior therapy, which was what the therapist (W. G.) had used in treating a friend of Paul's who had referred him to the author.

Paul was totally unable to give any information about the onset of his panic attacks or what triggered them. However, through self-monitoring, he was able to pinpoint that the panic attacks occurred in response to any manifestation of anxiety such as rapid heart rate, sweating, the warm sensation of adrenalin, headaches, and stomachaches. He also was able to identify negative self-statements such as "I can't handle these feelings; if they don't go away, I'll become helpless and out of control."

Because a search for external cues proved to be futile, the internal cues mentioned were used as items for desensitization therapy. As part of the desensitization procedure, Paul was relaxed and asked to imagine experiencing each of the sensations he feared. He was taught how to reduce his anxiety through the use of relaxation procedures and coping self-statements such as, "I can cope with anxiety. These sensations are uncomfortable but not dangerous. I don't have to totally eliminate the anxiety, just reduce it to a manageable level; it will pass." He was instructed to practice these techniques whenever he felt anxious. Paul reported some decrease in his anxiety as a result of his applying these procedures. However, after the 10th session, he requested hypnosis. He had seen a program on television in which a therapist had used hypnotic age regression to alleviate his patient's symptoms. Paul believed that he too had some deeply regressed memories that could only be retrieved through hypnotic regression and that he would not be cured until they were uncovered.

At first, the therapist encouraged Paul to continue with the desensitization, because he was making progress. However, at Paul's next session, he insisted that he was getting worse and that he was not getting the right treatment, which he believed was hypnotic regression. At this point, the therapist realized he had better join the resistance.

Hypnotic induction was easily accomplished through hand levitation. Paul was an excellent hypnotic subject and experienced spontaneous dissociation from his hands, which became anesthetized without his being given suggestions for numbness. Also during this first hypnotic session Paul was taught how to induce self-hypnosis through the same hand-levitation technique.

It was during Paul's second and last hypnotic session that he was trained in regression and was gradually brought back in time to the onset of his panic attacks. Hypnosis was induced through the *recall-induction technique* (Golden, 1986b). Through this procedure, hypnosis is induced by asking clients to recall in detail what they felt during their previous hypnotic experience. This procedure is ideal for preparing clients for regression, because it is itself an exercise in reexperiencing the past. The following dialogue took place between Paul and his therapist (reprinted in part from Golden, 1986b):

"Do you remember what you felt when you were experiencing hypnosis last week?"

"Yeah," he responded. "My arms started to feel light after I imagined a helium balloon under each of my hands."

At that point, Paul held out his arms in exactly the same position as he had the previous week when he experienced hand levitation. His arms were outstretched, and he held his hands just slightly above his thighs. The therapist continued the questioning.

"And what else did you experience?"

"My hands started to go numb," he replied.

Paul was already exhibiting a great deal of responsiveness to the procedure. His arms remained outstretched while the conversation continued. Paul appeared to be experiencing hand levitation as a result of recalling his previous experience with it. The therapist took Paul's high degree of responsiveness to the questioning as an indication that he would respond to direct suggestions to reexperience the past.

"And just as you experienced those sensations then, you can feel them again, now . . . just by recalling them. All you have to do is close your eyes, and go back in your mind to when you imagined those helium balloons . . . making your hands feel light and buoyant. . . . And what are you feeling now?"

"I, I feel it again. My hands feel light, and they're going numb. They feel like they're not attached to my body."

"Very good," the therapist reinforced Paul's responsiveness. "Now you can just let yourself go loose and limp. Letting yourself sink into the chair into a deep, deep hypnotic trance. . . . And whenever you want to go into a trance, all you have to do is just recall what it feels like to go into a trance, and you'll begin to reexperience those same feelings, the same sensations that you feel when you go into a deep trance. . . .

And in this trance your mind is very clear, and you can remember things very clearly, like this morning, when you were home, before you left your house. . . . Where are you?"

"I'm in the kitchen," he slowly uttered. "I'm at the table eating breakfast."

"What are you eating?"

"I'm having toast and some orange juice."

Once a pattern was established of having Paul describe the past as if he were actually there experiencing it, he was asked to go back further and further in time, 1 week ago, 1 month ago, 1 year ago, closer and closer to the time when his symptoms began. When the therapist thought Paul was close to that point in his life, he suggested, "And, as you already know, you are able to remember things when you are in a trance that you have repressed . . . memories, events, feelings that are related to your problem. . . . And you can tell me about them now . . . as you remember them."

Paul reported that his symptoms began after a bad LSD trip where he felt out of control and in a state of panic. The following was then suggested:

"And now Paul, that you are in a hypnotic state, you can reexperience those same sensations and perceptions that you did then when you were on that LSD trip. And you can feel confident that now you can master those feelings and overcome your fear of them. . . . You're going back, going back to that LSD trip . . . recalling what you felt on that trip . . . and, as you recall those sensations and perceptions, you will begin to reexperience them."

In response to these suggestions, Paul hallucinated that his hands disappeared and his body became distorted in size and shape. At first, he felt intense anxiety. However, with prolonged exposure (approximately 25 minutes), he was eventually able to experience the sensory and perceptual distortions without feeling anxious.

Next Paul was taught how to develop hypnotic control over sensory and perceptual distortions. It was suggested that his hallucinatory experiences would end. Then they were repeated once again through the same suggestion that he would reexperience them by recalling the sensations and perceptions that he experienced on the LSD trip. This symptom-utilization procedure (symptom induction and reduction) was repeated until the sensory and perceptual distortions could be reliably induced and removed.

Finally, Paul was taught to induce and remove the sensory and perceptual distortions on his own through self-hypnosis. Once he demonstrated that he could exercise control over these hallucinatory experiences and his anxiety symptoms, trance was terminated. At the next session, Paul reported that his symptoms were gone. Follow-up one year later indicated that he continued to be symptom-free.

## Case III

George was referred because of insomnia. He specifically requested hypnosis, stating that he had tried everything else and that it was his "last hope." He said that he had hardly slept at all for the past 4 months and insisted that he typically remained awake all night.

The therapist (E. T. D.) noticed immediately that George disagreed with almost everything he said. Sensing a reactant client, he felt that he was being set up to fail in using hypnosis. However, he agreed to try it in order to reduce the client's resistance.

The therapist induced a trance using the relaxation method and used a descent down a staircase as a deepening technique. Although the client did close his eyes when requested, he exhibited none of the other trance signs such as eyelid fluttering or loss of the swallow reflex. Later he stated that he wasn't really hypnotized because "I remember everything you said." This is a common statement from people who resist hypnosis.

At this point, the therapist directed George to deliberately remain awake all night every night for the next week to learn more about his insomnia. The following week George stated that he had slept all night for the first 2 nights and had thought his problem was solved. However, the remainder of the nights he had not slept at all and refused to try that technique again.

The therapist again joined the resistance and agreed with George that the trying-to-stay-awake strategy was obviously not appropriate for him. They discussed how George tried too hard to accomplish most things, including falling asleep. Objections by the client were met with the interpretation that they were more examples of his "trying too hard." The therapist then said that he would attempt to hypnotize him again but that it might not be successful because he would try too hard to be hypnotized. This is an example of the defiance-based strategy known as *inhibiting change*. The client was told that he could only be hypnotized if he did not try to be, thus placing him in a double bind. Hypnosis this time, again using the relaxation induction technique, was more successful. A hypnotic routine was conducted that stressed the double binding nature of anxiety and insomnia, in other words, the more anxious one becomes about not falling asleep, the less likely one is to fall asleep. The routine went as follows:

> And as you become more and more relaxed, not trying, not doing, you will be able to see more and more clearly how your anxiety about falling asleep prevents you from falling asleep. And as you continue not to try, you will find

it easier to fall asleep. The less you try, the more you will succeed, but the more you try, the less you will succeed.

The therapist also noted that George constantly derogated himself, for example referring to himself as a coward. This seemed to be a technique for putting himself down so that others would build him up by making positive comments about him. Using the paradoxical strategy of positioning (Dowd & Milne, 1986), the therapist spent several minutes discussing with George exactly what kind of a coward he was: a craven coward, an abject coward, or an occasional coward. This strategy elicited an objection from George that "I'm not *that* bad" and a wry admission that it had turned into a joke.

The next week George reported that he had slept through every night. When he became anxious, he repeated to himself "don't try" and fell asleep.

## DISCUSSION

These three cases illustrate how resistance can be overcome in hypnotherapy. In the first case, the resistance was anticipated and aborted before it developed. John was not given direct suggestions for trance induction, because other hypnotists had attempted to hypnotize him that way and failed. Instead the therapist preempted the resistance by agreeing that he could not hypnotize the client. By demonstrating a self-hypnotic procedure, the therapist was able to indirectly give John suggestions for relaxation and trance.

In the second case, the client's resistance was joined by utilizing hypnotic age regression, as the client had requested. Paul attributed his cure to his gaining insight through hypnotic age regression. The therapist, however, conceptualized the regression as a procedure that provided Paul with an opportunity to learn how to control the sensations that he feared. Despite the lack of a shared conceptualization of the problem and the treatment, Paul and his therapist were able to form an excellent collaboration. We believe this was because the therapist respected and utilized the client's wishes and ideas about how he should be treated.

In the third case, the therapist overcame the client's resistance by agreeing with him about his objections to treatment strategies. He also structured the hypnotic situation so that the client would have to take steps toward overcoming his problem (trying too hard) in order to enter a trance successfully. Resistance was also utilized by agreeing with the client about his cowardice, forcing him to adopt a different strategy to obtain positive comments.

# Chapter 9
# Self-Hypnosis Training

Whereas heterohypnosis is induced through a hypnotist, self-hypnosis is induced by the subject. Some investigators have focused on the differences between heterohypnosis and self-hypnosis; others have emphasized their similarities. Fromm et al. (1981), for example, maintained that imagery is richer in self-hypnosis, although one's attention is less focused than in heterohypnosis. They also found, in their research, that attempts to produce age regression and hallucinations were more successful through heterohypnosis. On the other hand, Ruch (1975) found that subjects responded to suggestions just as well under self-hypnosis. In another study, Johnson and Weight (1976) reported only minor differences between hetero- and self-hypnosis.

## THE COGNITIVE–BEHAVIORAL
## MODEL OF SELF-HYPNOSIS

Most cognitive–behavioral hypnotherapists (Araoz, 1981, 1982, 1985; Ellis, 1962; Golden, 1982) have emphasized the similarities between hetero- and self-hypnosis. From a cognitive–behavioral viewpoint, the distinction between heterohypnosis and self-hypnosis is useful only in describing who is initiating the process, hypnotist or subject. Barber and his associates (Barber, 1979; Barber et al., 1974; Spanos & Barber, 1976) have said that all hypnotic phenomena are the result of the same processes: the individual's motivation and cooperation, attitudes and expectations, and degree of absorption in suggestion-related thinking and imagining. Cognitive–behavioral therapists (Barber, 1979; Ellis, 1962) view the individual as ultimately responsible for the results in both hetero- and self-hypnosis. Ellis (1962) has stated that almost all hypnosis is the result of self-talk. In addition, Ellis (1962) and Araoz (1981, 1982, 1985) have said that neurotic suffering is due to an irrational, or negative, type of self-hypnosis. Maladaptive emotions and self-

119

defeating behavior are hypnotic in nature in that they stem from uncritical acceptance of one's negative self-suggestions. For example self-statements such as "I failed, therefore I'm worthless" lead to depression. Statements such as "I'm too weak to lose weight; I'll always be a fat person" are self-suggestions that prevent an individual from losing weight. In cognitive–behavioral hypnotherapy the client learns to replace these negative self-suggestions with more positive, constructive, and rational ones such as "I can still accept myself despite failure" and "I can lose weight; it might be hard at times, but I can do it."

# THE ERICKSONIAN MODEL OF SELF-HYPNOSIS

Erickson has also viewed self-hypnosis as involving the same basic phenomena as heterohypnosis. Erickson reported (see Rossi, Ryan, & Sharp, 1983) that his own self-discovery of autohypnosis occurred when he was a boy paralyzed from polio. He first experienced ideomotor functioning during his early attempts to overcome his paralysis. Left alone and tied into a rocking chair, he discovered that he could make the chair rock by thinking about its moving. Then, by recalling what sensations he had felt when he was capable of movement, he retrained himself to develop muscle control. For example, to regain use of his hands, he would stare at each hand for hours and recall the sensations that he had experienced when grasping objects. Gradually he developed increasingly more control over his body through these ideomotor procedures.

Whereas in cognitive–behavioral hypnotherapy clients are taught how to hypnotize themselves through specific self-control procedures, Erickson and his followers favor unconscious learning. Instead of teaching clients how to induce self-hypnosis through specific techniques such as concentrating on suggestion-related thoughts and images, Erickson has recommended a more unstructured experiential approach. According to the Ericksonian viewpoint, as a result of experiencing hypnotic phenomena, either through the help of a hypnotist or through self-discovery, the individual will have all of the learning experiences necessary to recreate the phenomena for himself or herself. However, neither Erickson nor any of his followers has clearly delineated how unconscious experiential learning takes place. They do make references to everyday experiences, like learning to walk or ride a bicycle, in which unconscious experiential learning occurs. They maintain that it is unnecessary to know how this learning takes place, only to trust that the unconscious knows more and can teach us more than we realize.

# INTEGRATING ERICKSONIAN AND COGNITIVE–BEHAVIORAL APPROACHES TO SELF-HYPNOSIS

There are advantages and disadvantages to each approach. The cognitive–behavioral approach has the advantage of providing clients, as well as clinicians, with specific guidelines to follow. By operationally defining self-hypnosis in terms of a series of steps, its mystery is removed, and it then becomes easier for clients to reproduce phenomena that they previously thought they could never control. Internal attributions for change are more likely to result under these conditions. Such internal attributions are more likely to produce enduring therapeutic results, as opposed to external attributions to a therapist, a drug, or "the powers of hypnosis."

On the other hand, some clients find the skills-training approach to self-hypnosis too structured or mechanistic for them. Some clients even object to having the mystery removed, as they expect and want hypnosis to have a certain mystique. These clients often resist rational and commonsense approaches. Several such cases can be found in the chapter on resistance. As noted in our discussion of resistance, it is very important for the clinician to remain flexible and sensitive to clients' expectations and to utilize them whenever possible. The strength of the Ericksonian approach lies in its flexibility and ability to handle a wide range of individual differences. However, the decision regarding which approach to use depends upon the client. Clients who prefer structure and rational, scientific explanations and methods do well with cognitive–behavioral approaches. Those who resist direction and structure and who are fascinated with the unconscious seem to do better with the Ericksonian approach.

In actual practice we frequently integrate elements from Ericksonian and cognitive–behavioral approaches. For example, in a structured training program, the client is taught a number of different self-hypnotic skills and techniques. Nevertheless, the client's preference and expectations can be utilized in developing an individualized program. The client selects which of the various methods he or she will employ.

Ericksonian principles can also be employed during heterohypnosis to explore how a client responds to various types of suggestions. After determining the client's response to particular suggestions, the hypnotist is in a position to make recommendations about what techniques and methods will be effective as self-hypnotic strategies. For example, a hypnotist could make use of open-ended suggestions such as the following:

And as one relaxes, it is possible to experience various sensations that accompany
the relaxation process. Some people begin to notice changes in their body

temperature . . . or their body weight. . . . You can just be aware of how you react.

There is a great deal of variation in how individuals respond to open-ended suggestions such as this. Some individuals experience lightness or heaviness, whereas others experience warmth or coolness. Some experience a combination of sensations. Despite these individual differences, there is usually consistency in how a given individual responds. Open-ended suggestions elicit response tendencies. That is why the use of open-ended suggestions increases the likelihood that the individual will respond in a way that is characteristic of him or her.

After employing open-ended suggestions to induce hypnosis, the hypnotist can ask the client what he or she experienced. Once the hypnotist knows how a client responds to a specific open-ended suggestion, he or she can be more direct during subsequent hypnotic inductions with this client. So, for example, if a client tends to experience heaviness and warmth to a set of open-ended suggestions for relaxation, then the hypnotist can be more direct and suggest that the client experience warmth and heaviness during the next hypnotic session. The hypnotist can also use this information to tailor the self-hypnosis training to fit the client's unique response tendencies. Learning about a client's response tendencies is like learning a formula. Once the formula for eliciting hypnotic phenomena in a given client is known, inducing hypnosis via heterohypnotic or self-hypnotic suggestion becomes more reliable and predictable.

# GOALS OF SELF-HYPNOSIS TRAINING

An important goal in therapy is for the client to eventually become his or her own therapist. Ideally, a client should terminate therapy with new coping skills and a greater sense of self-efficacy. Unfortunately, many hypnotists do not help clients in attaining this goal. Hypnosis can be presented in such a manner that subjects appear to be under the control of the hypnotist and seem to do things that they themselves could never do on their own. The result is a fostering of excessive dependency on the hypnotist. When clients attribute successful therapeutic outcomes to external causes such as a therapist, a drug, or hypnosis, therapeutic results are less likely to endure.

However, hypnosis can be an effective treatment with long-lasting results. Clients receiving hypnotherapy can be helped to develop confidence in their own ability to gain control over their lives. They can be taught how to reinforce therapeutic results obtained through the help of a therapist. In addition, many can be taught how to apply self-hypnosis to new problems that they can then treat themselves without the help of a therapist. It is through self-hypnosis training that hypnosis can be transformed into a self-management procedure.

## PREPARING CLIENTS FOR SELF-HYPNOSIS TRAINING

There is some debate about whether or not prior experiences with heterohypnosis interfere with the development of self-hypnotic skills. Ruch (1975) found that a prior heterohypnotic experience did interfere with subjects' progress in learning self-hypnosis. Ruch recommended training subjects in self-hypnosis before heterohypnosis. On the other hand, Johnson and Weight (1976) did not find that prior heterohypnotic experiences had a negative impact on self-hypnosis training. Clarke and Jackson (1983) claimed, on the basis of their clinical experience, that heterohypnosis has a facilitating effect on self-hypnosis. They recommended that the hypnotist begin with heterohypnosis before training a subject in self-hypnosis.

Another approach is to teach self-hypnosis at the time that one is training a client to respond to suggestions for heterohypnosis. In chapter 2 the hypnotic skills approach to teaching hypnotic responsiveness was outlined. The advantage of the hypnotic skills approach is that it facilitates the development of self-hypnotic skills, as well as hypnotic responsiveness in general. The client is taught how to respond to suggestions by focusing his or her attention and concentrating on suggestion-related thoughts and images, that is thoughts and images consistent with the goals of a suggestion. Through a series of structured exercises, as described in chapter 2, the client is first shown how to respond to very simple suggestions such as those for hand heaviness, hand levitation, and arm catalepsy. Then the client is taught step-by-step how to respond to progressively more difficult suggestions. Finally the client is taught how to formulate constructive suggestions and how to apply self-hypnosis to given situations.

## CLARIFYING MISCONCEPTIONS ABOUT SELF-HYPNOSIS

As discussed in chapter 2, there are certain fears and misconceptions about hypnosis that can interfere with treatment. Some of these fears are specific to self-hypnosis (Clarke & Johnson, 1983) and are listed here in addition to the misconceptions about hypnosis discussed in chapter 2.

### Self-hypnosis Is Dangerous

Do not assume that, if clients think that heterohypnosis is safe, they also feel the same about self-hypnosis. Some clients are hesitant to learn self-hypnosis because they fear that they might not be able to bring themselves out of it. Clients might not fear heterohypnosis because they feel confident that the therapist will be there to bring them out of trance.

These clients can be reassured by explaining to them that they will be able to terminate their trances upon their own commands. At the very worst, they might on occasion drift off into a natural sleep, in which case they will eventually wake up. Further reassurance can be given by having clients practice inducing and terminating self-hypnosis in the presence of the therapist before practicing it at home alone.

Another fear of some clients is that they will give themselves a suggestion, such as a hallucination, that will be harmful if not removed before termination of a trance. As Salter (1941) advised long ago, it is not necessary or wise to teach clients how to induce certain hypnotic experiences such as hallucinations. We would also recommend caution in teaching clients how to induce sensory alterations such as anesthesia, unless it is clear that their pain is not a symptom of some sort of undiagnosed medical problem.

## Self-hypnosis Cannot Be Used by Everyone

Another problematic misconception is the belief that only certain people are capable of using self-hypnosis. This belief is a simple misconception that can easily be clarified by explaining to clients that almost everyone can learn to use self-hypnosis, at least to some degree.

On the other hand, as in the case of Barbara, the belief that one is incapable of self-hypnosis can be symptomatic of a deeper sense of helplessness or feeling of inadequacy that pervades almost everything the client attempts. Such an individual has low self-efficacy (Bandura, 1977). In Barbara's case, it was pointed out that she typically underestimated her abilities in work, recreational, and social situations. She created a self-fulfilling prophecy, whereby she would, in effect, fail, not because of inadequacy, but because she avoided these situations out of fear of failure.

After Barbara was helped to recognize her self-defeating pattern, she agreed to take risks in order to overcome her fears. It soon became evident that she was much more capable than she realized. For instance, the therapist (W. G.) discovered that Barbara really knew how to start and maintain conversations but was afraid to risk making mistakes. Barbara was then encouraged to gradually put herself in more and more of the situations she avoided. In addition, an attempt was made to reduce her anxiety through hypnotic desensitization (see chapter 4). While in a relaxed state she was instructed to imagine herself dealing with progressively more and more anxiety-provoking situations. However, the desensitization was not generalizing to real-life situations. Even though she was confronting her fears and was being successful at work and meeting people, she was still quite anxious. She admitted that she was not practicing and applying self-hypnosis. She disclosed that she did not believe that she was capable of using self-hypnosis and was depending on the heterohypnosis to eliminate her anxieties. The familiar pattern of helplessness stemming from a feeling of inadequacy was pointed out to her.

Cognitive restructuring was used to help Barbara overcome her self-defeating pattern. The therapist suggested that she find out whether she really could or could not induce and use self-hypnosis, instead of automatically assuming that she could not. The therapist explained that, even if she were incapable of achieving certain goals, such as learning self-hypnosis or overcoming her social difficulties, that would not mean that she was a worthless or inadequate person. It would only prove that she was a fallible human being who was not perfect. The therapist also pointed out that much of her anxiety resulted from her making everything she attempted a measure of her self-worth.

To break Barbara's pattern of helplessness and avoidance, the therapist asked her to induce hypnosis in his presence. Much to her surprise she was successful. She was then willing to try inducing self-hypnosis with the therapist out of the room. Again she was successful and was given the assignment to practice at home. Finally, after she reported success at home practice, she was instructed to apply her self-hypnosis skills in the anxiety-provoking situations. As a result of this structured, step-by-step approach, Barbara's anxieties and feelings of helplessness were eventually reduced.

## METHODS OF SELF-HYPNOSIS

Salter (1941) has outlined three methods of self-hypnosis; the posthypnotic method, the memorization of self-hypnosis scripts, and "fractional" self-hypnosis. We offer the hypnotic-skills-training approach to self-hypnosis as an additional method.

### The Posthypnotic Method

A posthypnotic suggestion dealing with self-hypnosis can be given during heterohypnosis. The client is told prior to a trance induction that he or she will be given a posthypnotic suggestion that will enable him or her to enter self-hypnosis upon a given signal. We would recommend arranging in advance with the client what that signal will be. Salter (1941) used as a posthypnotic cue the suggestion that the client would take five deep breaths whenever he or she wished to enter hypnosis, and that, on the fifth breath, he or she would be in a deep trance. One advantage of using deep breathing as a cue is that it is itself a method of producing relaxation. However, any thought, image, or action can serve as a posthypnotic cue for self-hypnosis. One client, for example, used concentrating on the color blue as her cue.

Another client used her memory of the sound of sheets flapping in the wind as her cue. When she was a child, her bedroom window had been alongside the clothesline. She would lull herself to sleep by listening to the sound of the sheets flapping in the wind. Most clients seem to prefer single words, such as *relax*, *calm*, or *mellow*. At one time the word *sleep* was popular. Now most hypnotists discourage any association of hypnosis with sleep.

Clients need to be reassured that they will not slip into a trance if they or someone else should happen to say the cue word. Their fear of spontaneous trances can be alleviated through the following set of posthypnotic suggestions for self-hypnosis:

> From now on, whenever and wherever you wish to experience hypnosis, you will be able to do so by taking five long slow deep breaths. Each time you exhale, you will exhale very slowly and concentrate on the word, *calm* (or whatever word is chosen), and each time you exhale you will feel more relaxed. So that, by the fifth exhalation, you will be in a deep, relaxed, trancelike state, where you will be able to give yourself constructive suggestions. You will enter this state only when you want to. So if you or someone else mentions the word *calm*, or, if you think it, you will remain fully alert and wide awake. Only when you wish to go into trance and purposely use your signal will you enter hypnosis. And when you wish to return to the fully alert, wide-awake state, all you have to do is count to three and suggest as you count that you will return to the wide-awake alert, state, opening your eyes, feeling refreshed, relaxed, and wide awake.

Before termination of the trance, the client is given an additional posthypnotic suggestion that, after his or her eyes open, he or she will induce self-hypnosis through the posthypnotic cue. The hypnotist can thereby monitor the client's first experience with self-hypnosis. Furthermore, successful execution of the posthypnotic suggestion to induce self-hypnosis reinforces the client's belief in the ability of hypnosis to induce change. However, do not assume that, because a client responds to a posthypnotic suggestion to reinforce trance, he or she will be able to do so again without the therapist's being present. In Barbara's case, she responded to the posthypnotic cue initially but was not able to do it on her own.

## Self-hypnosis Scripts

Clients can be given self-hypnosis scripts to memorize after they have experienced heterohypnosis. There are some individuals who are able to learn self-hypnosis through scripts without first experiencing heterohypnosis. However, many individuals seeking hypnotherapy are looking for direction. They expect the hypnotist to do most of the work and often resist learning self-hypnosis. Hence, it is very important that the hypnotist guide them very carefully. The use of tape recordings can be very helpful in providing clients with a smooth transition from hetero- to self-hypnosis. Tapes made during therapy sessions are preferable to prerecorded tapes of hypnotic inductions, because the former can be tailored to the client's preferences, expectations, and pacing. The length of time of the tape depends on the client. After several heterohypnotic experiences, clients usually know how long they need to achieve a state of hypnosis that is comfortable for them. The same is true for the length of time a client should spend practicing self-hypnosis. Most clients seem to prefer 5, 10, or 15 minutes. However, as they develop more skill as a result of practice, the amount of time can be shortened to achieve the same results. After clients have had some success with heterohypnosis, printed material can then be given to them, so that they can make their own hypnosis tapes. The following printed material is given to clients and self-hypnosis workshop participants.

## Hypnotic Induction Techniques

There are many different hypnotic induction techniques. Four will be described here for the purpose of self-hypnosis; the relaxation method, the eye-fixation technique, the hand levitation method, and the hand heaviness method. Experiment and discover which works for you.

*Exercise 1: The Relaxation method.* Imagery, breathing techniques, and suggestions of relaxation may all be employed as part of the relaxation method. The induction that follows is written in the first person. However, in phrasing your suggestions for self-hypnosis, you may address yourself as "You" or "I." "I am relaxed" and "You are relaxed" are equally effective. You may either tape-record the following transcript, memorize it, or have someone read it to you.

First find a comfortable place to practice in a room free from distractions. You may either sit or lie down. Close your eyes and listen to the following instructions:

My eyes are closed. I'm going to take five deep breaths in order to start the relaxation. One, inhaling slowly and deeply, and then exhaling slowly and deeply. Sinking into the chair as I exhale. Two, again filling my lungs with air, fully, and then exhaling, letting all of the air out and letting go of tension. Three, another long, slow, deep, breath and exhale, let go, and relax. Each time I exhale, I can feel more relaxed. Four, inhaling, a long slow, deep, breath, all the way, and then exhale. Just relax. Let the tension flow out. One more time. Five, inhale, Fill the lungs with air, and then exhale slowly and deeply. Feel the relief from exhaling. Feel the relaxation spreading all over.

And now, my pleasant relaxing scene. I'll just let my mind drift off into a pleasant relaxing fantasy. Seeing it. Hearing it. Feeling it. Smelling it. Even tasting it if I can. Use all of the senses. Just keep on imagining a calm, serene scene. If my mind wanders, I'll just let it wander to other pleasant thoughts and fantasies. . . . And I feel myself becoming more relaxed.

My whole body is becoming relaxed. My arms and legs are relaxing. Feet relaxing. Toes relaxing. Calves, knees, and thighs becoming relaxed. All of my limbs are loose and limp, becoming more and more relaxed. My jaw is hanging slack, teeth slightly parted, lips slightly parted. Facial muscles becoming relaxed. Neck hanging in a comfortable position. Shoulder hanging loose and limp. Back loose and limp. The chest muscles are relaxing. Stomach muscles relaxing.

And I feel other pleasant sensations as I feel the relaxation spreading throughout my body. Becoming more and more relaxed. I feel my whole body slowing down, becoming calm and comfortable, loose and limp. All the muscles relaxing more and more.

My arms and legs becoming more relaxed. Facial muscles smooth and relaxed. Jaw hanging slack. Neck relaxed. Shoulders in a comfortable position. Back loose and limp. Chest relaxed. Breathing slowly and comfortably. A slow, deep, rhythmic breathing pattern. More and more relaxed. Stomach muscles becoming more relaxed. Just letting go of any remaining tension . . . . Now I will deepen the trance further and give myself constructive suggestions. (See the sections on deepening techniques and trance utilization. You may employ these procedures at this point before terminating your trance.)[1] (pause)

In a few moments, after I finish giving myself constructive suggestions, I will open my eyes, feeling wide awake, relaxed, and refreshed in mind and body.

*Exercise 2: Eye-fixation.* The goal of the eye fixation is to induce a trance by creating a feeling of heaviness in the eye muscles and eyelids. Although it is not necessary, usually eye closure is also a goal. You may tape the following instructions or have someone read them to you. Eventually you will be able to use eye fixation on your own to enter a trance. You may reword the instructions and put them in the first person.

Select an object, like a spot on the wall or ceiling, a flickering flame of a candle, a light, or a ring on your finger as a target. Stare at the target. If your eyes should wander, just go back to staring at the same object. Keep on staring at the object until your eyes become tired of it. Then just let your eyes close so you can begin to relax.

Many people report visual distortions during eye fixation. The target may seem as if it was moving. It may change color, or disappear. There may be a fogging of the visual field. The target may become fuzzy. Your eyes will probably begin to feel heavy, tired, so heavy that they feel like closing. Or you may feel drowsy, tired, feel like closing your eyes and entering a peaceful relaxed state of mind. Feel yourself starting to relax.

Your breathing will start to slow down; a slow, deep, rhythmic breathing. You're becoming more relaxed, more drowsy. But you do not fall asleep, just feeling more relaxed. Calm and relaxed. Body becoming loose and limp. Feel the relaxation spreading, all over, more and more. (Now you may deepen the trance further. Employ one or several of the procedures from the section on deepening techniques. (pause)

Now you can give yourself constructive suggestions. (See the section on

---

[1]If you record this transcript on tape, leave a few minutes of blank tape here for deepening procedures, followed by therapeutic suggestions and imagery. Alternatively, instead of leaving blank space, record the instructions and suggestions you want to give yourself.

formulating hypnotic suggestions.) (pause) In a few moments, after giving yourself constructive suggestions, you will open your eyes, feeling wide awake, relaxed, and refreshed.

*Exercise 3: Hand levitation and hand heaviness.* Hand levitation and hand heaviness may be used separately or together. When used together, hold both arms parallel out in front of you. Close your eyes and suggest that one arm becomes light and lifts while the other becomes heavy and lowers. Imagine something that would make one of your arms light if it were really happening, such as imagining that a balloon is attached to your hand. Imagine that you are holding something very heavy in your other hand to create a feeling of heaviness. Once you get a response, and your arm levitates to suggestions of lightness or lowers to suggestions of heaviness, give yourself suggestions of relaxation or drowsiness and say to yourself "Now I am entering a trance." Deepen the trance by using one or two of the techniques from the next section. Then give yourself constructive suggestions before terminating your trance.

## Deepening Techniques

Once you have induced a hypnotic trance you may proceed to deepen it through further suggestions. Induction techniques can also be used interchangeably as deepening techniques. For example, if you employ hand levitation as an induction procedure, you can use the relaxation method as a deepening technique, and vice versa. Likewise, one may induce trance through eye fixation and then deepen the trance through suggestions of relaxation.

Several other deepening techniques will now be described. Use the ones that are most effective for you and that you feel comfortable using. Wait until after you have deepened your trance before giving yourself constructive suggestions.

*Exercise 4: Heaviness.* Suggest that various parts of your body begin to feel heavy. Then suggest a sinking sensation. For example "My body feels so heavy that I feel myself sinking into the chair deeper and deeper. And the deeper I sink the more relaxed I become. I feel myself sinking into a deep trance." Remember to reverse the suggestions of heaviness before you terminate your trance. Suggest that your body feels its normal weight and is no longer feeling heavy.

*Exercise 5: Lightness.* You may suggest lightness instead of heaviness. But do not use both since they counteract one another. Suggest that the lighter your body becomes the more relaxed you feel. You may also suggest that your body feels so light that you feel as if you are floating or drifting off into a deep, deep trance.

*Exercise 6: Warmth.* As you become more relaxed your arms and legs tend to warm up. Focusing on this phenomenon can enhance the effect and deepen relaxation. You may also create feelings of warmth through imagery, such as imagining being near a fireplace and feeling the warmth of the fire radiating and warming your hands and legs.

*Exercise 7: Breathing.* Concentrate on your breathing. Breathe slowly and deeply. Suggest that, with each exhalation, you are going into a deeper state of relaxation or trance.

*Exercise 8: Counting.* Slowly count up to a certain specific number, like 10 or 20. Suggest, in between counts, that each number helps you go into a deeper trance or helps you become more relaxed.

*Exercise 9: Relaxation imagery.* Utilize relaxation imagery to deepen your trance. As an example, imagine that you are walking in the woods and you come upon a stream. Suggest that the sound of the stream makes you feel relaxed.

*Exercise 10: Stairway image.* Imagine that you are walking down a long stairway and suggest that with each step you take you are entering a deeper state of hypnosis.

*Exercise 11: Hourglass image.* Imagine an hourglass, or a minute glass, and imagine the grains of sand falling from the top to the bottom. Suggest that as each grain of sand falls you will go into a deeper and deeper trance.

*Exercise 12: Black-dot image.* Imagine a small black dot on a white background. Imagine that black dot growing larger and eventually consuming the entire field. Suggest that the larger the black dot grows, the deeper your trance becomes.

*Exercise 13: Music.* Imagine listening or actually listen to your favorite, soft, relaxing music. Suggest that the music will deepen you relaxation or trance.

## How to Formulate Hypnotic Suggestions

During trance you can give yourself constructive suggestions, modify negative and irrational thinking, and employ therapeutic imagery. You can increase your motivation by reminding yourself of your goals, the reasons why you wish to attain them, and can imagine yourself going through the various steps you need to take in order to attain these goals. Here are six general principles that can be used in the construction of most hypnotic suggestions.

*Use positive wording.* Whenever possible use positive wording in the construction of your suggestions. It is better to suggest "I can and will quit smoking" than "I won't smoke." However, be realistic. It is unrealistic to expect positive suggestions to perform magic or miracles. Therefore, suggestions such as "I will always be totally relaxed" or "I will definitely do great at the interview and get the job" are to be avoided.

Keep in mind that sometimes the only way to word a suggestion is with some negative wording. One such example might be "It doesn't mean I'm a failure or worthless if I act anxious or if I fail to get the job." These suggestions are effective because they counter negative irrational beliefs such as "I am a worthless person if I fail."

*Use an image as well as a suggestion.* Suggestions are more effective when you use imagery. So, for example, in addition to suggesting that you will lose weight, imagine yourself eating less, resisting snacks, refusing seconds, and finally losing weight.

*Make your suggestions flexible.* Change your demands to preferences. Avoid "musts" and "shoulds." People often rebel when they are told, or tell themselves, what they "must" do. Therefore avoid giving yourself rigid authoritarian commands such as "I will never smoke another cigarette for the rest of my life." This type of suggestion is unrealistic and creates needless anxiety and self-downing should you fail to succeed perfectly and quickly. A more flexible permissive suggestion would be "I will become more and more in control over my desire to smoke as I learn to relax and cope with stress."

*Allow time for change.* Usually changes in behavior occur over a period of time and in small incremental steps. Keep this in mind when you are formulating suggestions. Instead of demanding that you change your eating habits or stop smoking overnight give yourself suggestions that permit time to take place. For instance a suggestion that allows for time would be "As I continue to practice self-hypnosis and imagine myself with better eating habits, I will eat less and less fattening foods and lose more and more weight."

*Repetition.* In addition to allowing time for change, repeat your suggestions again and again until they do have an effect. A negative form of self-hypnosis occurs when individuals give themselves negative suggestions such as "I'll never succeed. I can't change." These negative self-defeating suggestions have been repeated a countless number of times, often without your awareness. In order to counteract the effect of this "Negative Self-hypnosis," it is important to repeat constructive suggestions as many times as you can. You can give yourself these suggestions during your self-hypnosis practice sessions at home and also at other times throughout the day. Give yourself pep talks anytime, and anywhere, especially in the problematic situation itself. For example, when you feel tempted to eat a high-caloric dessert, say to yourself, at that moment, "I can be in control. I've had enough to eat. I can turn down the dessert even if it is my favorite."

People often assume that if they give themselves a positive suggestion under self-hypnosis or receive a posthypnotic suggestion from a hypnotist it will continue to affect them indefinitely. They do not realize that one can easily counteract constructive suggestions with negative thinking. That is why it is important to be aware of one's "Negative Self-hypnosis" and to recognize when you are giving yourself negative self-defeating suggestions. Considering that negative suggestions can always return, repeat constructive suggestions as much as possible in order to weaken the effect of the old negative ones. Also, whenever negative or irrational thoughts return, neutralize them by once again repeating your constructive suggestions.

*Avoid suggestions that imply failure or doubt.* When constructing suggestions avoid words that imply failure, doubt, and lack of follow-through such as "I hope I stick to my diet," or "I'll try to give up cigarette smoking." One does not hope, wish, or try to do things that are within one's control. You either do them or not. When people say or tell themselves they will try to do something, they usually do not do it. Therefore, give the power back to yourself and suggest "I will accomplish my goals, I may backslide at times, but I am basically moving forward and can control my eating, smoking. . . ."

## Terminating the Trance

One may terminate trance through suggestions such as "I will now open my eyes feeling wonderful, relaxed, refreshed, wide awake, and alert." The counting method is another approach. One counts forward to a specific number, such as from one to five, or one to ten, or one can count backwards from a number, such as from five to zero. During the count, suggestions of wakefulness and alertness are given. Remember to remove any suggestions, such as feelings of heaviness, that you do not want to remain.

## Summary of the Self-hypnotic Procedure

*Hypnotic-trance induction.* Practice inducing self-hypnosis through the relaxation method, eye fixation, hand levitation, and/or hand heaviness.

*Deepening techniques.* Once you can induce a trance, practice deepening it with the various deepening techniques.

*Trance utilization.* Once you can induce and deepen trance and have constructed therapeutic suggestions and imagery, you are ready to utilize trance. Six principles that can be employed in developing constructive suggestions are 1) use positive wording whenever possible, 2) use imagery, 3) make your suggestions flexible, 4) allow time for suggestions to have an effect, 5) repeat suggestions as many times as possible and whenever needed, and 6) avoid suggestions that imply doubt or failure.

*Terminating the trance.* Use the counting method or simply suggest termination.

## The Fractional Self-Hypnotic Method

Salter (1941) has compared the fractional self-hypnosis method to the part method of learning, or, what behavior therapists now call *successive approximations*. The learning of self-hypnosis is broken down into a series of discrete parts.

Salter begins with the *body sway* suggestion. The client stands, and the hypnotist suggests "you're falling forward." The suggestion is repeated until the client falls forward and is caught by the hypnotist. After the client responds, the hypnotist explains that it does not matter who gives the suggestion, whether it is the hypnotist or the person himself or herself. Then the hypnotist has the client repeat the falling forward suggestion to herself or himself. The hypnotist catches the client as he or she falls forward.[2]

Other *waking* suggestions, or, suggestions without a prior trance induction, are then given to the client. The format is the same. After the client responds to the waking suggestion of the hypnotist, he or she then uses self-suggestion to produce the same effects. Salter employs Chevreul's pedulum (see chapter 2), arm and leg catalepsy, and finally body heaviness and relaxation. As a result of going through this series of successive approximations, the client learns to self-induce the various phenomena associated with hypnosis.

## The Hypnotic Skills Training Method

The hypnotic skills approach is similar to the fractional method of teaching self-hypnosis. The major difference is theoretical. Salter's (1949) explanation of hypnosis is in terms of conditioned reflexes, whereas the hypnotic skills approach is based on a cognitive–behavioral paradigm. Nevertheless, many

---

[2]We do not recommend this exercise unless the hypnotist is quick enough and strong enough to catch the client.

of the same techniques and concepts are employed, such as the method of successive approximations, the use of suggestions without a prior trance induction, and the stressing of the importance of concentration and cooperation.

Chapter 2 contains a detailed description of a hypnotic skills training procedure, which can be used to teach self-hypnosis and to increase hypnotic responsiveness in general. After teaching the client how to concentrate and how to use cognitive strategies such as imagery and self-suggestion, the therapist guides the client through a heterohypnosis experience. The heterohypnosis provides the client with a model of what to do when he or she practices self-hypnosis. Any hypnotic induction procedure can be used. However, it is to be preferred that either the client chooses the method of induction or the therapist picks an induction procedure that matches the client's response tendencies. Previously we discussed how open-ended suggestions can be used to elicit these response tendencies. We also discussed in chapter 2 how the hypnotic skills training procedure can be used in a similar fashion. Each exercise in the procedure (such as hand heaviness and lightness and arm catalepsy) provides the therapist and the client with information regarding the responsiveness of the client to each type of suggestion. A decision about which induction procedure to use can be made on the basis of how the client responds to the various exercises. For example, a client who is responsive to suggestions of lightness and hand levitation will do well with a hand-levitation induction procedure. Eye fixation and heaviness would not be used as an induction procedure for a client who was more responsive to suggestions of lightness than suggestions of heaviness.

After the client has successfully completed the skills training and has experienced heterohypnosis, the therapist can either provide the client with scripts such as the ones from this chapter or simply encourage the client to induce self-hypnosis by employing the skills he or she learned. When this sequence of hypnotic skills training, heterohypnosis, and self-hypnosis practice is followed, it is not necessary to give posthypnotic suggestions for self-hypnosis. However, some clients still prefer to receive suggestions for self-hypnosis while "under" heterohypnosis.

## CLINICAL APPLICATION OF SELF-HYPNOSIS

A case will now be presented that illustrates many of the principles and procedures discussed in this chapter.

Arnold was referred for hypnotherapy for a facial tic. He made turtlelike gestures with his jaw that others noticed, although he was unaware of them. It seemed to occur when he was anxious, but it also occurred when he was concentrating on activities like watching television, or solving a business problem, or playing with his 3-year-old daughter. He requested hypnosis even though another hypnotist had been unsuccessful in treating the tic. His request was honored. In addition, electromyographic (EMG) biofeedback equipment was used during the first session to assess Arnold's baseline level of jaw tension and to demonstrate to him how to tense and let go of jaw tension. Massetter muscle baseline readings ranged from 45 mu to 50 mu. Because Arnold was almost totally unaware of the tic, massed practice (Yates, 1958) of the tic was prescribed. Arnold was instructed to ask his wife to demonstrate the tic. After careful study of the exact movements involved in the tic, he was to practice it while observing himself in a mirror. Once a day he was to engage in massed practice of the tic to the point of exhaustion. He reported that he had had to practice the tic for approximately half an hour before he felt fatigue and discomfort.

At Arnold's second session, self-hypnosis training was initiated. He was receptive to learning self-hypnosis, which he had not learned from his previous hypnotist. Arnold's prior experience with hypnotherapy was limited to his receiving posthypnotic suggestions to not engage in the tic. Although he was an excellent hypnotic subject, the hypnotic skills training procedure was employed anyway, to demonstrate to him that his responsiveness was due to skills that he possessed and was not caused by some external agent.

Arnold was most responsive to suggestions of heaviness and stated a preference for the eye-fixation induction procedure. This was also the method of induction used by the previous hypnotist. During hypnosis, it was suggested that

> From now on you are going to become more and more aware of when your jaw is tense, even before you begin to distort your face (the client's own words in describing his problem). And as soon as you notice this tension, you will begin to enter self-hypnosis by taking five long slow deep breaths. . . . And with each exhalation your jaw will relax more and more. . . . And the rest of your body will also relax more and more, just as you are doing now. Just letting go of the tension and entering a very relaxed state all over.

Before Arnold's trance was terminated, he was given the additional suggestion that, after he opened his eyes, he would reinduce hypnosis on his own by staring at a spot and taking five long, slow deep breaths and would relax more and more with each exhalation. Arnold successfully self-induced a hypnotic state, during which the therapist asked him to imagine himself in various situations, noticing his jaw tension and relaxing the tension away through self-hypnosis. He was instructed to practice this imagery exercise at home during his self-hypnotic practice. He was also told, while he was still in this self-induced hypnotic state, that he would begin to do in reality what he was now imagining himself do while hypnotized.

The following week Arnold returned, reporting that he had never been so aware of the high levels of tension in his jaw. He wondered whether the hypnosis had caused his tension to increase. It was explained that people often are unaware of how tense they actually are until they learn to relax. He was also told that the first step for him was to be more aware of that tension, as well as to be more aware of when he was engaging in the tic. Arnold reported that he practiced the self-hypnosis exercises at home and had already begun to apply the self-hypnotic relaxation procedure whenever he was aware of the tension. He seemed to feel that the frequency of the tic had diminished and got feedback from his wife and friend that he was, in fact, doing it less. Arnold returned for three more sessions. Each week he reported feeling less jaw tension and a reduction in the frequency of the tic. EMG massetter baseline readings were down to a range of 6 mu to 8 mu. By using his self-hypnotic skills alone, without feedback, Arnold was able to reduce his jaw tension to 4 mu. Arnold was satisfied with the control that he had over the tic, and therapy was terminated.

## SUMMARY

In this chapter the rationale and goals of self-hypnosis were presented. Various methods of self-hypnosis were described. The sequence of steps in implementing a self-hypnosis training program was outlined, and a clinical example was offered.

# Afterword

We have presented in this book a broad-based treatment that encompasses traditional, cognitive–behavioral, and Ericksonian hypnotherapy methods. The integrated approach that we have described is modern in that it includes strategies and techniques derived from contemporary methods of hypnotherapy and those derived from the more traditional methods. Specifically, cognitive–behavioral and Ericksonian techniques have been heavily utilized in the book.

Because of its recent appearance on the therapeutic scene, there has been little research to date on the efficacy of cognitive–behavioral hypnotherapy. The limited data that does exist, as well as clinical experience, suggest that it is effective, especially in teaching the client coping strategies and making him or her a therapeutic collaborator.

A similar situation exists for Ericksonian hypnotherapy. Although Milton Erickson practiced his unique brand of hypnotherapy for many years in obscurity, it is only recently that a significant number of clinicians have practiced Ericksonian hypnotherapy. In addition, because of the complexity of its methods, controlled research has been extremely difficult to conduct. We hope that this book will enable clinicians to apply Erickson's strategies and researchers to evaluate them. We have attempted to isolate and operationalize some of what we consider to be Erickson's most clinically useful techniques and have attempted to remove some of the mystery surrounding Ericksonian hypnotherapy. Research is needed to evaluate the effect of an integration of cognitive–behavioral and Ericksonian hypnosis with more traditional approaches.

We recognize that some clinicians might object to our combination of methods from diverse schools. We believe, however, that it is important for clinicians to be willing to employ whatever techniques are effective instead of whatever corresponds to their theoretical orientation. Theoretical schools of all sorts are currently on the wane, and integration is increasing.

Our intention has been to describe how we do hypnotherapy and to encourage others to experiment with it. Rather than apply these techniques in a mechanical, rote fashion, we suggest that you integrate the methods described in this book into your own style in a way that is comfortable for you. We think it is undesirable for any clinician to "go by the book," whether it be our book or any other book.

When three diverse professionals write a book together, there is a danger that they could be perceived by the readers as thinking and practicing alike. That is an example of the "uniformity myth" that has been increasingly recognized as false. The reality is that, although there are important commonalities in our separate approaches, there are also significant differences. What we have in common is our integration of traditional, cognitive–behavioral, and Ericksonian approaches; our differences lie in the relative mix of these approaches and in our own individual styles. Fortunately, the commonalities outweigh the differences, or we could not have written this book at all! To allow readers to distinguish each author's individual therapeutic style and relative mix of theoretical approaches, we have identified the therapist in each of the cases. Our purpose was to give the flavor of the diverse ways in which it is possible to conduct hypnotherapy. It is hoped that, this will assist others in applying the material in this book in a manner consistent with their own styles.

We hope this "therapeutic odessey" has been useful and that readers will feel comfortable utilizing hypnosis in their clinical work.

# Appendix

PERSONAL ATTITUDE INVENTORY

Instructions: Please answer each item by circling the appropriate answer.

SD = Strongly disagree   D = Disagree   A = Agree   SA = Strongly agree

1. If I receive a lukewarm dish at a restaurant, I make an attempt to let that be known. SD D A SA
2. I resent authority figures who try to tell me what to do. SD D A SA
3. I find that I often have to question authority. SD D A SA
4. I enjoy seeing someone else do something that neither of us are supposed to do. SD D A SA
5. I have a strong desire to maintain my personal freedom. SD D A SA
6. I enjoy playing "devil's advocate" whenever I can. SD D A SA
7. In discussions, I am easily persuaded by others. SD D A SA
8. Nothing turns me on as much as a good argument! SD D A SA
9. It would be better to have more freedom to do what I want on a job. SD D A SA
10. If I am told what to do, I often do the opposite. SD D A SA
11. I am sometimes afraid to disagree with others. SD D A SA
12. It really bothers me when police officers tell people what to do. SD D A SA
13. It does not upset me to change my plans because someone in the group wants to do something else. SD D A SA
14. I don't mind other people's telling me what to do. SD D A SA
15. I enjoy debates with other people. SD D A SA
16. If someone asks a favor of me, I think twice about what this person is really after. SD D A SA
17. I am not very tolerant of others' attempts to persuade me. SD D A SA

HMA-K

| | | | | |
|---|---|---|---|---|
| 18. | I often follow the suggestions of others. | SD | D | A | SA |
| 19. | I am relatively opinionated. | SD | D | A | SA |
| 20. | It is important to me to be in a powerful position relative to others. | SD | D | A | SA |
| 21. | I am very open to solutions to my problems from others. | SD | D | A | SA |
| 22. | I enjoy "showing up" people who think they are right. | SD | D | A | SA |
| 23. | I consider myself more competitive than cooperative. | SD | D | A | SA |
| 24. | I don't mind doing something for someone even when I don't know why I'm doing it. | SD | D | A | SA |
| 25. | I usually go along with others' advice. | SD | D | A | SA |
| 26. | I feel it is better to stand up for what I believe than to be silent. | SD | D | A | SA |
| 27. | I am very stubborn and set in my ways. | SD | D | A | SA |
| 28. | It is very important for me to get along well with the people I work with. | SD | D | A | SA |

## HOW TO USE THE SCALE

The Therapeutic Reactance Scale (TRS) is easy to score. Simply assign a value of 4 to Strongly Agree, 3 to Agree, 2 to Disagree, and 1 to Strongly Disagree. This scoring should be reversed for the reverse-keyed items (Items 7, 11, 13, 14, 18, 21, 24, 25, 28). Then add up the numbers for the 28 items for the total score. The minimum possible score is 28 (low reactance) and the maximum possible score is 112 (high reactance).

To use the TRS scores, it is important to know how they compare with others' scores. The scale was given to 211 educational psychology undergraduates at a large midwestern university. For this sample, the mean score was 66.68, the median score was 66.50, the standard deviation was 6.59, and the total range was 46 to 83. Although you can use these scores to compare your individual scores to, we would also encourage you to collect your own comparative data for the people with whom you typically work.

The TRS seems to measure the independent construct of psychological reactance. It has negligible correlations with the Counselor Rating Form (a measure of therapist social influence), the Beck Depression Inventory, and the Spielberger State-Trait Anxiety Inventory. On the other hand, it correlates positively with an internal locus of control, which would be expected, according to the theory of psychological reactance. Research has shown that high-reactant people tend to show less change in procrastination and anxiety after treatment than low-reactant people. In addition, in one study, high-reactant clients had a higher no-show rate and a longer duration of treatment than low-reactant clients.

# References

Araoz, D. L. (1981). Negative self-hypnosis. *Journal of Contemporary Psychotherapy, 12,* 45–52.

Araoz, D. L. (1982). *Hypnosis and sex therapy.* New York: Brunner/Mazel.

Araoz, D. L. (1984). Hypnosis in the treatment of sexual dysfunctions. In W. C. Wester II & A. H. Smith, Jr (Eds.), *Clinical hypnosis: A multidisciplinary approach.* Philadelphia: Lippincott.

Araoz, D. L. (1985). *The new hypnosis.* New York: Brunner/Mazel.

Bandler, R. , & Grinder, J. (1975). *Patterns of the hypnotic techniques of Milton H. Erickson, M.D.* Cupertino, C. A.: Meta Publications.

Bandura, A. (1977). Self-efficacy: Toward a unifying theory of behavioral change. *Psychological Review, 84,* 191–215.

Banyai, E. I., & Hilgard, E. R. (1976). A comparison of active-alert hypnotic induction with traditional relaxation induction. *Journal of Abnormal Psychology, 85,* 218–224.

Barber, T. X. (1979). Suggested ("hypnotic") behavior: The trance paradigm versus an alternative paradigm. In E. Fromm & R. E. Shor (Eds.), *Hypnosis: Developments in research and new perspectives* (2nd ed.). New York: Aldine.

Barber, T. X. (1984). Hypnosis, deep relaxation, and active relaxation: Data, theory and clinical applications. In R. L. Woolfolk & P. M. Lehrer (Eds.), *Principles and practice of stress management.* New York: Guildford Press.

Barber, T. X., Spanos, N. P., & Chaves, J. F. (1974). *Hypnosis, imagination and human potentialities.* Elsmford, NY: Pergamon Press.

Beck, A. T. (1976). *Cognitive therapy and the emotional disorders.* New York: International Universities Press.

Beck, A. T., & Emery, G. (1985). *Anxiety disorders and phobias: A cognitive perspective.* New York: Basic Books.

Beck, A. T., Hollon, S. D., Young, J. E., & Bedrosian, R. C. (1985). Treatment of depression with cognitive therapy and amitriptyline. *Archives of General Pschiatry, 42,* 142–148.

Beck, A. T., Kovacs, M., & Weissman, A. (1975). Hopelessness and suicidal behavior: An overview. *Journal of the American Medical Association, 234,* 1146–1149.

Beck, A. T., Rush, A. J., Shaw, B. F., & Emery, G. (1979). *Cognitive therapy of depression.* New York: Guildford.

Beck, A. T., Weissman, A., Lester, D., & Trexler, L. (1974). The measurement of pessimism: The Hopelessness scale. *Journal of Consulting and Clinical Psychology, 42,* 861–865.

Bernheim, H., (1895). *Suggestive therapeutics.* New York: Putnam's.

Blackburn, I. M., Bishop, S., Glen, A. I. M., Whalley, L. J., & Christie, J. E. (1981). The efficacy of cognitive therapy in depression: A treatment trial using cognitive therapy and pharmocotherapy, each alone and in combination. *British Journal of Psychiatry, 139,* 181–189.

Brehm, J. W. (1966). *A theory of psychological reactance.* New York: Academic Press.

Cautela, J. R. (1967). Covert sensitization. *Psychological Reports, 74,* 459–468.

Chiasson, S. W. (1973). *A syllabus on hypnosis.* American Society of Clinical Hypnosis, Education, and Research Foundation.

Clarke, C. J., & Jackson, J. A. (1983). *Hypnosis and behavior therapy: The treatment of anxiety and phobias.* New York: Springer.

Crasilneck, H. B., & Hall, J. A. (1985). *Clinical hypnosis: Principles and applications* (2nd ed.) New York: Grune & Stratton.

Davison, G. C., Tsujimoto, R. N., & Glaros, A. G. (1973). Attribution and the maintenance of behavior change in falling asleep. *Journal of Abnormal Psychology, 82,* 124–133.

Diamond, M. J. (1974). Modification of hypnotizability: A review. *Psychological Bulletin, 81,* 180–198.

Diamond, M. J. (1977). Hypnotizability is modifiable: An alternative approach. *International Journal of Clinical and Experimental Hypnosis, 25,* 147–166.

Dowd, E. T., & Milne, C. R. (1986). Paradoxical interventions in counselling psychology. *The Counselling Psychologist, 14*(2), 237–282.

Dowd, E. T., Milne, C. R., & Wise, S. L. (1984, August). *The Therapeutic Reactance Scale: Development and reliability.* Paper presented at the meeting of the American Psychological Association, Toronto, Canada.

Dunn, R. J. (1979). Cognitive modification with depression-prone psychiatric patients. *Cognitive Therapy and Research, 3,* 307–317.

Ellis, A. (1962). *Reason and emotion in psychotherapy.* New York: Lyle Stuart.

Erickson, M. H. (1952). A therapeutic double bind utilizing resistance. In E. L. Rossi (Ed.) (1980), *The collected papers of Milton H. Erickson on hypnosis, Vol. IV.* New York: Irvington.

Erickson, M. H., & Rossi, E. L. (1979). *Hypnotherapy: An exploratory casebook.* New York: Irvington.

Erickson, M. H., Rossi, E. L., & Rossi, S. L. (1976). *Hypnotic realities.* New York: Irvington.

Ferster, C. B. (1973). A functional analysis of depression. *American Psychologist, 28,* 857–870.

Festinger, L., & Maccoby, N. (1964). On resistance to persuasive communications. *Journal of Abnormal and Social Psychology, 68,* 359–366.

Fordyce, W. L. (1974). Treating pain by contingency management. In J. J. Bonica (ed.), *Advances in neurology: Vol. 4.* New York: Raven Press.

Freud, S. (1920). *A general introduction to psychoanalysis.* New York: Washington Square Press.

Friday, N. (1973). *My secret garden: Women's sexual fantasies.* New York: Simon & Schusterr, Pocket Books.

Fromm, E., Brown, D. P., Hurt, S. W., Oberlander, J. Z., Boxer, A. M., & Pfeifer, G. (1981). The phenomena and characteristics of self-hypnosis. *The International Journal of Clinical and Experimental Hypnosis, 29*(3), 189–246.

Fuller, J. (1981). *Rational stage-directed hypnotherapy in the treatment of self-concept and depression in a geriatric nursing home population: A cognitive experiential approach.* Unpublished doctoral dissertion, Ohio State University.

Gallagher, E. B., & Wrobel, S. (1982). The sick-role and chronic pain. In R. Roy & E. Runks (Eds.), *Chronic pain: Psychosocial factors in rehabilitation.* Baltimore: Williams & Wilkins.

Gargiulo, T. (1983). *Influence of training in hypnotic responsivity on hypnotically suggested analgesia.* Unpublished doctoral dissertation, California Coast University, CA.

Gold, M. S., Pottash, A. L. C., Extein, I., & Sweeney, D. R. (1981). Diagnosis of depression in the 1980s. *JAMA, 245,* 1562–1564.

Golden, W. L. (1982). *Self-hypnosis: The rational-emotive approach* [Cassette Recording]. New York: Institute for Rational-Emotive Therapy.

Golden, W. L. (1983a). Rational-emotive hypnotherapy: Principles and techniques. *British Journal of Cognitive Psychotherapy, 1*(1), 47–56.

Golden, W. L. (1983b). Resistance in cognitive-behaviour therapy. *British Journal of Cognitive Psychotherapy, 1*(2), 33–42.

Golden, W. L. (1986a). Can hypnotized patients be persuaded to do almost anything? In B. Zilbergeld, M. G. Edelstien, & D. L. Araoz (Eds.), *Hypnosis: Questions and answers.* New York: Norton.

Golden, W. L. (1986b). An integration of Ericksonian and cognitive-behavioral hypnotherapy in the treatment of anxiety disorders. In E. T. Dowd & J. M. Healy (Eds.), *Case studies in hypnotherapy.* New York: Guilford Press.

Golden, W. L., & Dryden, W. (1986). Cognitive–behavioural therapies: Commonalities, divergencies and future developments. In W. Dryden & W. L. Golden (Eds.), *Cognitive–behavioural approaches to psychotherapy.* London: Harper & Row.

Golden, W. L., & Friedberg, F. (1986). Cognitive-behavioural hypnotherapy. In W. Dryden & W. L. Golden (Eds.), *Cognitive-behavioural approaches to psychotherapy.*

Golden, W. L., Friedberg, F., & Richman, D. (1983). The winning edge. *New Body, 2,* 47, & 78–80.

Golden, W. L., & Mills, R. (1982). *The sexual realities project: A self-help approach.* New York: Academic Visual Productions.

Haley, J. (1973). *Uncommon therapy: The psychiatric techniques of Milton Erickson, M.D.* New York: Ballantine.

Haley. J. (1976). *Problem-solving therapy.* San Francisco: Jossey-Bass.

Healy, J. M., & Dowd, E. T. (1986). Hypnotherapeutic control of long-term pain. In E. T. Dowd & J. M. Healy (Eds.), *Case studies in hypnotherapy.* New York: Guilford Press.

Hilgard, E. R. (1968). *The experience of hypnosis.* New York: Harbinger.

Johnson, L. S. & Weight, D. G. (1976). Self-hypnosis versus heterohypnosis: Experiential and behavioral comparisons. *Journal of Abnormal Psychology, 85,* 523–526.

Kaplan, H. S. (1979). *Disorders of sexual desire.* New York: Brunner/Mazel.

Kaplan, H. S. (1983). *The evaluation of sexual disorders.* New York: Brunner/Mazel.

Katz, N. W. (1979). Comparative efficacy of behavioral training, training plus relaxation, and sleep/trance hypnotic induction in increasing hypnotic susceptibility. *Journal of Consulting and Clinical Psychology, 47,* 119–127.

Kelly, F. D., Dowd, E. T., & Duffey, D. K. (1983). A comparison of cognitive and behavioral intervention strategies in the treatment of depression. *British Journal of Cognitive Psychotherapy, 1*(2), 51–58.

Kroger, W. S., & Fezler, W. D. (1976). *Hypnosis and behavior modification: Imagery conditioning.* Philadelphia: Lippincott.

Lazarus, A. A. (1968). Learning theory and the treatment of depression. *Behavior Research and Therapy, 6,* 83–89.

Lazarus, A. A. (1973). "Hypnosis" as a facilitator in behavior therapy. *International Journal of Clinical and Experimental Hypnosis, 21,* 25–31.

Lazarus, A. A., & Fay, A. (1982). Resistance or rationalization. In P. L. Wachtel (Ed.), *Resistance.* New York: Plenum Press.

Lewinsohn, P. M. (1974). A behavioral approach to depression. In R. M. Friedman & M. M. Katz (Eds.). *The psychology of depression: Contemporary theory and research.* New York: Wiley.

Marlatt, G. A., & Gordon, J. R. (1980). Determinants of relapse: Implications for the maintenance of behavior change. In F. C. Davidson & S. M. Davidson (Eds.). *Behavioral medicine: Changing health life-styles.* New York: Brunner/Mazel.

Masters, W., & Johnson, V. (1970). *Human sexual inadequacy*. Boston: Little, Brown.

Meichenbaum, D., & Gilmore, J. B. (1982). Resistance from a cognitive-behavioral perspective. In P. L. Wachtel (Ed.). *Resistance*. New York: Plenum Press.

Melzack, R., & Wall, P. D. (1965). Pain mechanisms: A new theory. *Science, 150*, 971–979.

Orne, M. T., & Evans, F. J. (1965). Social control in the psychological experiment: Antisocial behavior and hypnosis. *Journal of Personality and Social Psychology, 1*(3), 189–200.

Prince, M., & Coriat, I. (1907). Cases illustrating the educational treatment of the psychoneuroses. *Journal of Abnormal Psychology, 2*, 166–177.

Rossi, E. L. (Ed.). (1980). *The collected papers of Milton H. Erickson on hypnosis*. New York: Irvington.

Rossi, E. L., Ryan, M. O., & Sharp, F. A. (Eds.). (1983). *Healing in hypnosis: The seminars, workshops, and lectures of Milton H. Erickson, Vol. 1*. New York: Irvington.

Ruch, J. C. (1975). Self-hypnosis: The result of heterohypnosis or vice versa? *International Journal of Clinical and Experimental Hypnosis, 23* 282–304.

Rush, A. J., Beck, A. T., Kovacs, M., & Hollon, S. (1977). Comparative efficacy of cognitive therapy and pharmacotherapy in the treatment of depressed outpatients. *Cognitive Therapy and Research, 1*, 17–37.

Salter, A. (1941). Three techniques of autohypnosis. *Journal of General Psychology, 24*, 423–438.

Salter, A. (1949). *Conditioned reflex therapy*. New York: Capricorn.

Spanos, N. P., & Barber, T. X. (1974). Toward a convergence in hypnosis research. *American Psychologist, 29*, 500–511.

Spanos, N. P., & Barber, T. X. (1976). Behavior modification and hypnosis. In M. Hersen, R. M. Eisler, & P. M. Miller (Eds.). *Progress in behavior modification*. New York: Academic Press.

Turk, D. C., Meichenbaum, D., & Genest, M. (1983). *Pain and behavioral medicine: A cognitive-behavioral perspective*. New York: Guilford Press.

Wadden, T. A., & Anderton, C. H. (1982). The clinical use of hypnosis. *Psychological Bulletin, 91*, 215–243.

Watkins, J. G. (1951). A case of hypnotic trance induced in a resistant subject in spite of active opposition. *British Journal of Medical Hypnosis, 2*, 26–31.

Watzlawick, P. (1978). *The language of change: Elements of therapeutic communication*. New York: Basic Books.

Watzlawick, P., Weakland, J., & Fisch R. (1974). *Change: Principles of problem formation and problem resolution*. New York: Norton.

Weitzenhoffer, A. M. (1963). *Hypnotism*. New York: Wiley: Science Editions.

Weitzenhoffer, A. M. (1972). Behavior therapeutic techniques and hypnotherapeutic methods. *American Journal of Clinical Hypnosis, 15*, 71–82.

Wolpe, J., & Lazarus, A. A. (1968). *Behavior therapy techniques*. Elmsford, NY: Pergamon Press.

Yates, A. J. (1958). The application of learning theory to the treatment of tics. *Journal of Abnormal and Social Psychology, 56*, 175–182.

Young, P. C. (1927). Is rapport an essential characteristic of hypnosis? *Journal of Abnormal and Social Psychology, 22*, 130–139.

# Author Index

Anderton, C. H., 6,74
Araoz, D. L., 3, 5, 9, 13, 32, 51, 71, 86, 91, 99, 119

Bandler, R., 21, 22
Bandura, A., 124
Banyai, E. I., 35
Barber, T. X., 5, 6, 8, 13, 119
Beck, A. T., 31-32, 33, 45
Bedrosian, R. C., 32
Bernheim, H., 1
Bishop, S., 32
Blackburn, I. M., 32
Brehm, J. W., 100

Cautela, J. R., 97
Chaves, J. F., 8
Chiasson, S. W., 26
Christie, J. E., 32
Clarke, C. J., 11, 123
Coriat, I., 1
Crasilneck, H. B., 24, 85

Davison, G. C., 14
Diamond, M. J., 4
Dowd, E. T., 39, 66, 101, 109, 110, 118
Duffey, D. K., 39
Dunn, R. J., 32

Ellis, A., 31, 32, 119
Emery, G., 30, 45, 46
Erickson, M. H., 2, 5-6, 11, 20, 21-23, 100, 106, 107, 111, 112, 120
Evans, F. J., 12
Extein, I., 31

Fay, A., 100
Ferster, C. B., 36
Festinger, L., 106
Fezler, W. D., 3, 24
Fisch, R., 110
Fordyce, W. L., 60
Freud, S., 2
Friday, N., 92
Friedberg, F., 34, 74
Fromm, E., 119
Fuller, J., 31

Gallagher, E. B., 60
Gargiulo, T., 4, 64
Genest, M., 61
Gilmore, J. B., 102
Glaros, A. G., 14
Glen, A. I. M., 31
Gold, M. S., 31
Golden, W. L., 12, 14, 23, 34, 41, 74, 92, 101, 108, 113, 115, 119
Gordon, J. R., 105
Grinder, J., 21, 22

Haley, J., 100, 105, 111
Hall, J. A., 24, 85
Healy, J. M., 66
Hilgard, E. R., 13, 35
Hollon, S. D., 31-32

Jackson, J. A., 11, 123
Johnson, L. S., 119, 123
Johnson, V., 85, 87

Kaplan, H. S., 86, 88, 89
Katz, N. W., 4
Kovacs, M., 31, 33

147

Kroger, W. S.,   3, 24

Lazarus, A. A.,   10, 37, 100
Lester, D.,   33, 37
Lewinsohn, P. M.,   36

Maccoby, N.,   106
Marlatt, G. A.,   105
Masters, W.,   85, 87
Meichenbaum, D.,   61, 102
Melzack, R.,   58, 61
Mills, R., 92
Milne, C. R.,   101, 109, 110, 118

Orne, M. T.,   12

Pomerleau, O. F.,   102
Pottash, A. L. C.,   31
Prince, M.,   1

Richman, D.,   34
Rossi, E. L.,   2, 5, 21, 106, 107, 120
Rossi, S. L.,   107
Ruch, J. C.,   119, 123
Rush, A. J.,   30, 31
Ryan, M. O.,   120

Salter, A.,   3, 11, 124, 125, 133
Sharp, F. A.,   120
Shaw, B. F.,   30
Spanos, N. P.,   13, 119
Sweeney, D. R.,   31

Trexler, L.,   33
Tsujimoto, R. N.,   14
Turk, D. C.,   61

Wadden, T. A.,   6, 74
Wall, P. D.,   58, 61
Watkins, J. G.,   13
Watzlawick, P.,   105, 110, 112
Weakland, J.,   110, 111
Weight, D. G.,   119, 123
Weissman, A.,   33
Weitzenhoffer, A. M.,   3, 12, 13
Whalley, J. A.,   31
Wise, S. L.,   101
Wolpe, J.,   100
Wrobel, S.,   60

Yates, A. J.,   135
Young, J. E.,   31-32
Young, P. C.,   11, 13

# Subject Index

Age regression, 54-57, 115-117
Age revivification, 54
Alert hypnosis, 6, 8, 35-36
Analgesia, anesthesia, hypnotic, 68-69
Anxiety, fear, phobias and stress
  distinctive features, 45
  functions of, 46
  stress-related symptoms, 47
  treatment of, 47-57

Case examples
  anxiety, 50-51, 53-54, 55-57
  depression, 37-39, 41-44
  habit control, 81-84
  pain control, 71-72
  sexual dysfunction, 91-99
  resistance, 112-118
  self hypnosis, 134-135
Chiasson's method of hypnotic
  induction, 26-27
Cognitive restructuring
  for anxiety, 52-54
  for depression, 41-49
  for habit disorders, 77
  for pain control, 70-71
  for sexual dysfunction, 94-95

Deepening techniques
  counting techniques, 28
  in self-hypnosis, 129-130
  stairway image, 27-28
Depression
  biochemical, 30-31
  diagnosis and assessment, 33-35
  psychological, 31-33
  symptoms, 30
  treatment of, 35-44

Desensitization, hypnotic, 49-51, 93-94
Direct methods for overcoming
  resistance, 108-109
Direct suggestion, as pain
  treatment, 66
Dissociative techniques, as pain
  treatment, 69
Distraction, as pain treatment, 69-70

Ericksonian techniques, 20-24

Fear, see Anxiety

Habit disorders
  assessment of, 75
  situational factors in, 75-77
  treatment techniques, 77-81
Hypno-assertion, 96-97
Hypnotic aversion treatment, 97-99
Hypnotic regression, 54-57, 115-117
Hypnotherapeutic approaches
  cognitive-behavioral
    hypnotherapy, 3-4
  Ericksonian hypnotherapy, 2-3
  hypnoanalysis, 2
  hypnobehavioral model, 3
  hypnotic skills training, 4, 14-18, 64, 133-134
  similarities of technique among
    models, 6
  traditional hypnosis, 1-2
Hypnotherapy, modern, 4-7
  cooperation and motivation, 4-5
  indications for, 6-7
  insight-orientated, 54-57
  for anxiety, fears, phobias and
    stress, 48

thinking and imagining,   5-6
Hypnotic induction,   8, 18-19
   clarifying misconceptions about,
      11-14
   eye fixation/hand heaviness
      method,   25-26
   in self-hypnosis,   127-129
   pacing and joining,   10
   rapport during,   9-11
   relaxation method,   24-25
   skills training for,   14-18
   standard procedures,   24-27
   utilizing clients' responses,   19
   utilizing expectations and
      preferences,   19
Hypnotic relaxation, as pain
   treatment,   65-66
Hypnotic skills training,   4, 14-18, 64,
   133-134

Imaginal rehearsal,   43
   for habit disorders,   77-80
   for sexual dysfunction,   95-96
Indirect methods, for overcoming
   resistance,   109
Indirect suggestions, as pain
   treatment,   66

Pacing and leading,   3, 6, 10
Pain
   acute,   61
   assessment of,   62-64
   behavioral factors in,   60
   chronic, intractable, benign,   61
   chronic, periodic,   61
   cognitive factors in,   59
   emotional factors in,   59-60
   general treatment of,   64-65
   interpersonal factors in,   60
   perceptual factors in,   58
   specific treatments,   65-71
Paradoxical interventions,   109-110
Phobias, see Anxiety

Resistance,   100-118
   sources of,   101-102
   strategies for overcoming,   109-112
   strategies for preventing,   102-107

Self-hypnosis
   clarifying misconceptions about,
      123-125
   clinical application,   134-136
   cognitive-behavioral model of,
      119-120
   Ericksonian model of,   120
   for habit disorders,   80-81
   goals of,   122-123
   integration of models in,   121-122
   negative,   3, 13, 32, 39, 51, 52, 71,
      86
   preparing clients for,   123
Self-hypnosis methods,   125-134
   formulating suggestions for,
      130-132
   fractional method,   133
   post-hypnotic method,   125-126
   scripts for,   126-127
Sex therapy, traditional,
   limitations of,   85-86
   intergration with hypnosis,   86
Sexual dysfunction
   assessment/differential
      diagnosis,   88-91
   dyadic factors in,   87-88
   psychological factors in,   88
   treatment techniques,   91-99
Stress, see Anxiety

Time projection technique,   36-37
Trance termination,   28-29, 132
Transformation of pain,   67-68
Two-column method,   41

Uncovering techniques,   39-41, 52
   evocative imagery,   40-41, 91
   self-monitoring,   39

# About the Authors

William L. Golden received his PhD in psychology from the New School for Social Research in New York City in 1975. He did a postdoctoral fellowship at the Institute for Rational–Emotive Therapy in New York City, where he is presently the Director of Behavior Therapy Training. He is also the Associate Director of the Institute for Behavior Therapy in Westchester, is on the faculty of Cornell Medical College, and has a private practice in New York City and in Briarcliff Manor, New York.

Dr. Golden is a member of the American Psychological Association, the Westchester County Psychological Association, the Association for the Advancement of Behavior Therapy, and the Phobia Society of America. He is on the editorial boards of the *Journal of Cognitive Psychotherapy: An International Quarterly* and the *Journal of Rational-Emotive Therapy*. He is the coeditor of *Cognitive-Behavioural Approaches to Psychotherapy* and has authored articles and chapters on hypnosis, cognitive–behavioral therapy, biofeedback, stress management, and sports psychology. He also has produced educational films on stress management and sex therapy.

E. Thomas Dowd received his PhD in counselling psychology from the University of Minnesota in 1971. He has worked as a Veterans Administration Medical Center psychologist, served as a University Counseling Center psychologist, and taught at Florida State University and the University of Nebraska. He is currently Professor and Director of Counseling Psychology Training at Kent State University.

Dr. Dowd is a Fellow of the American Psychological Association (Division 17); a Diplomate in Counseling Psychology, American Board of Professional Psychology, Inc.; and a member of the Society for Clinical and Experimental Hypnosis. He is coeditor of the *Journal of Cognitive Psychotherapy: An International Quarterly*.

Fred Friedberg, PhD, received his doctorate in psychology at the City University of New York. He maintains a private practice in Huntington and Stony Brook, New York. Dr. Friedberg has authored articles on hypnosis, stress management, and sport psychology.

151

# Psychology Practitioner Guidebooks

Editors
Arnold P. Goldstein, Syracuse University
Leonard Krasner, Stanford University & SUNY at Stony Brook
Sol K. Garfield, Washington University

Elsie M. Pinkston & Nathan L. Linsk – CARE OF THE ELDERLY: A Family
Approach

Donald Meichenbaum – STRESS INOCULATION TRAINING

Sebastiano Santostefano– COGNITIVE CONTROL THERAPY WITH
CHILDREN AND ADOLESCENTS

Lillie Weiss, Melanie Katzman & Sharlene Wolchik – TREATING BULIMIA:
A Psychoeducational Approach

Edward B. Blanchard & Frank Andrasik – MANAGEMENT OF CHRONIC
HEADACHES: A Psychological Approach

Raymond G. Romanczyk – CLINICAL UTILIZATION OF
MICROCOMPUTER TECHNOLOGY

Philip H. Bornstein & Marcy T. Bornstein – MARITAL THERAPY: A
Behavioral-Communications Approach

Michael T. Nietzel & Ronald C. Dillehay – PSYCHOLOGICAL
CONSULTATION IN THE COURTROOM

Elizabeth B. Yost, Larry E. Beutler, M. Anne Corbishley & James R. Allender
– GROUP COGNITIVE THERAPY: A Treatment Method for Depressed
Older Adults

Lillie Weiss – DREAM ANALYSIS IN PSYCHOTHERAPY

Edward A. Kirby & Liam K. Grimley – UNDERSTANDING AND TREATING ATTENTION DEFICIT DISORDER

Jon Eisenson – LANGUAGE AND SPEECH DISORDERS IN CHILDREN

Eva L. Feindler & Randolph B. Ecton– ADOLESCENT ANGER CONTROL: Cognitive-Behavioral Techniques

Michael C. Roberts – PEDIATRIC PSYCHOLOGY: Psychological Interventions and Strategies for Pediatric Problems

Daniel S. Kirschenbaum, William G. Johnson & Peter M. Stalonas, Jr. – TREATING CHILDHOOD AND ADOLESCENT OBESITY

W. Stewart Agras – EATING DISORDERS: Management of Obesity, Bulimia and Anorexia Nervosa

Ian H. Gotlib & Catherine A. Colby – TREATMENT OF DEPRESSION: An Interpersonal Systems Approach

Walter B. Pryzwansky & Robert N. Wendt – PSYCHOLOGY AS A PROFESSION: Foundations of Practice

Cynthia D. Belar, William W. Deardorff & Karen E. Kelly – THE PRACTICE OF CLINICAL HEALTH PSYCHOLOGY

Paul Karoly & Mark P. Jensen – MULTIMETHOD ASSESSMENT OF CHRONIC PAIN

William L. Golden, E. Thomas Dowd & Fred Friedberg – HYPNOTHERAPY: A Modern Approach

Patricia Lacks – BEHAVIORAL TREATMENT FOR PERSISTENT INSOMNIA

Arnold P. Goldstein & Harold Keller – AGGRESSIVE BEHAVIOR: Assessment and Intervention

C. Eugene Walker, Barbara L. Bonner & Keith L. Kaufman – THE PHYSICALLY AND SEXUALLY ABUSED CHILD: Evaluation and Treatment

Robert E. Becker, Richard G. Heimberg & Alan S. Bellack – SOCIAL SKILLS TRAINING TREATMENT FOR DEPRESSION